PHOEBE FARAG MIKHAIL

Putting *Joy* into Practice

SEVEN WAYS
TO LIFT YOUR SPIRIT
FROM THE
EARLY CHURCH

PARACLETE
PRESS
Brewster, Massachusetts

2019 First Printing

Putting Joy into Practice: Seven Ways to Lift Your Spirit from the Early Church

Copyright © 2019 Phoebe Farag Mikhail

ISBN 978-1-64060-168-0

Library of Congress Cataloging-in-Publication Data

Names: Mikhail, Phoebe Farag, 1978- author.
Title: Putting joy into practice : seven ways to lift your spirit from the early church / Phoebe Farag Mikhail.
Description: Brewster, MA : Paraclete Press, Inc., 2019. | Includes bibliographical references.
Identifiers: LCCN 2018048176 | ISBN 9781640601680 (trade paper)
Subjects: LCSH: Christian life—Coptic Church authors. | Christian literature, Early.
Classification: LCC BX137.15 .M554 2019 | DDC 248.4/6—dc23
LC record available at https://lccn.loc.gov/2018048176

10 9 8 7 6 5 4 3 2 1

Published by Paraclete Press
Brewster, Massachusetts
www.paracletepress.com
Printed in the United States of America

To my children, Mercurius, Mariam, and Abadir,
who teach me something about joy every day.

To my husband, Fr. Bishoy Lamie Mikhail,
and to my parents, Fr. Athanasius Farag and Soher Farag,
who have modeled the spiritual disciplines joyfully.

With great joy from
Higher Ground ECYC 2019,

Phoebe
Farag
Mikhail

CONTENTS

Invitation

f "happiness is a warm blanket," as Linus proclaims in the *Charlie Brown* cartoons, then joy is a walk with a dear friend. I'd like to invite you on that walk with me. We'll take a path that I'm familiar with, so I can point out a few twists and turns you may not see. We'll start early in the morning and take breaks along the way. We'll stop and help others along the path, and perhaps they might join our walk. I'll share what I've learned on this walk so far, as well as lessons I've learned from those who have walked this way before me. We'll talk about joy, and we'll try to understand it, experience it, and share it with others.

I started this journey of joy accidentally. An overheard conversation planted a question inside me that refused to let me go until I could find some answers to it. In that conversation, an elder advised a friend to focus during the Resurrection season on joy.

"That's easy enough," she replied.

"No," he said. "It's not that easy."

This response surprised me. Why is living in joy so hard? What can we do to live in the joy of the Resurrection when there are so many ways our joy can be stolen? As I pondered these questions, they led me on a path of trying to learn why joy is so hard, but more importantly, to learn how to live in joy, how to protect it from the thieves that strive to steal it, and how to share it with others.

I considered ancient wisdom, the tried and true knowledge of the ages. I joined others on their walks, learning from them the practices that helped them live in and share their joy. I struggled myself with joy, losing it and finding it, losing it again, and finally realizing I can only really keep the joy I find if I give it away.

I invite you to join me on this walk, this path to joy that, providentially for us, has been beaten well before us. Centuries ago, three people took a similar walk together, two of them not yet realizing they were on a path to joy—until they reached a stop on their journey and sat down to eat. There they discovered that, on the road to Emmaus, they were walking with joy. There they discovered they had been walking with the Risen Christ himself.

CHAPTER

One

What Is Joy?

In the beginning there are a great many battles and a good deal of suffering for those who are advancing towards God and afterwards, ineffable joy. It is like those who wish to light a fire; at first they are choked by the smoke and cry, and by this means obtain what they seek (as it is said: "Our God is a consuming fire" [Heb. 12.24]): so we also must kindle the divine fire in ourselves through tears and hard work.

—AMMA SYNCLETICA, *Sayings of the Desert Fathers*

The night had finally arrived. Fifty-five days of fasting, and a week of walking with Christ through his pain, struggle, humiliation, torture, and death had led up to this, the Divine Liturgy celebrating the feast of feasts: our Lord Jesus Christ's resurrection from the dead.

We gathered that Saturday evening, dressed in our finest, filled with excitement and anticipation. The church was similarly adorned: the curtains in front of the altar, usually red, but dressed in black during Pascha Week,[1] had been changed to bright white curtains embroidered with images of the victorious risen Lord. The hymns had transformed from the somber tones of Good Friday to the joyous tones of the Feast of the Resurrection. Everyone, no matter what mood they were in before walking through the doors, was infected with the joyous celebration enveloping us in church that night.

The highlight of the Resurrection Liturgy in the Coptic Orthodox Church of Alexandria is an "enactment" of the Resurrection at midpoint. The priest closes the curtains in front of the altar and shuts off all the lights in the church. The darkness is lit only by the small candles in the hands of the chanters standing in front of the closed curtain. The priest stands inside the altar, on the other side of the curtain, and together they begin singing a dialogue that goes like this:

    Priest: Christ is risen; indeed he is risen.
  Chanter: Open your doors, O you kings,
            and be lifted up,
            you everlasting doors,
            that the King of Glory may come in (Psalm 24:7).
    Priest: Who is the King of Glory?
  Chanter: The LORD, majestic, strong, powerful,
            mighty in battles, he is the King of Glory!
            (Psalm 24:8).

In the darkness, the priest and the chanter repeat the first two lines three times before the question, "Who is the King of Glory?"

On this night, Andrew was the chanter. Andrew, in his twenties, is the oldest of three boys. He was born with a chromosomal deletion that was supposed to cause him severe mental retardation. He behaves on the autism spectrum, was born with a cleft palate, and is deaf in one ear. He also has an exceptional ability to learn the most complicated and melodic Coptic hymns—including all the microtones and melasmas that make Coptic hymns notoriously difficult to memorize—and a powerful voice that can carry any tune.

My heart soared with Andrew's voice as it resounded in response to the question, "Who is the King of Glory?" "He is, He is the King of Glory!" he sang. I had goosebumps imagining our Lord rolling away the stone and rising, victorious, from the tomb. I was also thinking about Andrew, and how God's amazing work in him and his family had transformed what seemed on the outside like an adult with special needs to one of the most talented chanters in our church. Andrew's life is a story of resurrection and its joy.

I turned my head for a moment and noticed that behind me, Maryann was standing, also engrossed in the dramatic dialogue unfolding in front of us in the dark. A month before, Maryann watched as her seventeen-year-old younger sister Michelle was struck by a car and killed while crossing the street in front of their home. Michelle was just about to graduate from high school and was headed for a seven-year medical program. Her sudden death affected all of us. I remember walking into the church a few hours after Michelle's funeral, before a memorial service was to start. Although I was the only person in the sanctuary, somehow, as I stood in front of her photograph surrounded by fragrant flowers, I could feel her presence still.

On this night I wanted to whisper to Maryann, "Christ is risen." *Christ is risen* means *Michelle will also be risen*, because Michelle loved him in ways we could all see, through her service and witness to others and through her everyday kindness. I didn't get Maryann's attention, but she heard those words the very next minute.

After Andrew's last chant of "He is, He is the King of Glory," the lights burst on, a thunderous sound roared, and the chanters, the priests, and the congregation erupted in the hymn *"Christos Anesti,"* with the words "Christ is risen from the dead, trampling down death by death, and upon those in the tombs bestowing life!" Priests, deacons, and chanters started their procession around the church with the icon of our resurrected Lord, as members of the congregation reached out to touch the icon for a kiss as it passed. Children joined in, too, and if there weren't so many people, we all might have joined.

As the procession continued, I noticed an elderly woman sitting in the back, smiling, her hands perpetually trembling. Her daughter, herself a mother of three children, stood beside her, singing along with the chanters in the procession, also smiling. Later during the Liturgy, the priest would carry Communion to the elderly woman, and her daughter would photograph her. She does it every time she's able to bring her mother to church. Sometimes I wonder if she does this so the photographs will be a comfort for her when her mother eventually passes away, a memory of seeing her united with Christ on earth in the Eucharist when she is united with Christ in heaven.

This daughter might be called a member of the "sandwich generation," caring for an elderly parent while still caring for her own children—and working outside the home to alleviate the financial burden.[2] But there, during the Resurrection procession, she didn't seem to be worried about how she and her sons will wheel her mother back into her car to drive home, how she'll prepare an Easter feast for her family later, how she'll pay her son's college tuition, and how she'll have energy for work on Monday morning. She's singing "Christ Is Risen" along with the rest of us, joyful that Christ has conquered death and given us eternal life.

Experiencing the joy of the Resurrection in the face of life's daily struggles can be difficult. Experiencing the joy of the Resurrection in the face of the challenges of raising a special needs child—or any child, for that matter—can be almost impossible. Experiencing the joy of the Resurrection in the wake of the sudden death of a loved one is almost too much to ask. Yet it is perhaps for this reason that we are reminded that this is a joyous season and offered ways to experience it.

For the fifty days after the Resurrection Feast, even funerals are prayed with the joyful tune. The casket is processed into the church with this same hymn, "Christ Is Risen" rather than the more somber tone of "Remember Me O Lord," which is sung on Good Friday and during funerals for the rest of the year. I harbor a secret hope that when I pass away, I might pass away during the Holy Fifty Days.

It is remarkable but characteristic that the Coptic Orthodox Church of Alexandria, which is mostly known for its martyrs and for the strict ascetic practices of its desert monasteries, infuses its rites and practices with daily reminders to be joyful. In his *Introduction to the Coptic Orthodox Church*, Fr. Tadros Malaty observes:

> Almost all the days are feasts to the Coptic Church. Although she is known for bearing the cross, she is eager to have her children live in the midst of sufferings in spiritual gladness. She is capable, by the Lord's help, to raise them above tribulations. In other words, the Coptic Church is continuously suffering and joyful at the same time, her feasts are uninterrupted, and her hymns with a variety of melodies are unceasing.[3]

My son recognized this at age five as we were on our way to church. He asked, "What's today's feast?" I had not yet checked the day's readings to find out what saint we might be commemorating, but I remembered that it was Sunday. "On Sunday," I told him, "we always celebrate the Feast of the Resurrection." The Feast of the Resurrection, the feast of feasts, lasts liturgically not just on Easter Sunday itself, but for fifty days thereafter, until Pentecost. The Resurrection is celebrated every Sunday of the year, not just Easter Sunday, commemorated daily in the morning prayer of the *Agpeya*, which is the Coptic Daily Office, and commemorated monthly on the 29th of each Coptic month.[4]

Now, don't misunderstand me. The people in my church have as many problems as anyone else you might meet on a given day. At any feast is a collection of hurting, struggling people, called to find joy in the promises of the Resurrection despite what life throws at them. And finding and living in that joy is not an easy task, so the church provides us with these reminders—joyous tunes even during funerals, bright white curtains, and no fasting for fifty days after the Resurrection Feast. These help us to live the feast not just for one night, but for weeks.

Those weeks are my favorite time of the year. Even as a child, I preferred the Easter season to Christmas. In the Northern Hemisphere, Easter coincides with spring, with flowers, with beauty and life, as if nature itself were singing its joyous hymns of Resurrection with us. Yet for a long time, I confused joy with happiness, and sometimes with pleasure, as many of us do. Easter means Resurrection, but it also once meant chocolate, cheese, chicken—everything I couldn't eat during the Great Lent. Those are pleasures, but they don't bring joy. If unfettered access to food brought joy, we North Americans should be the most joyous people on earth, rather than battling depression and anxiety. Joy is not pleasure, and in fact, joy can be lost in excessive pleasure.

Easter also meant family, a feast that brought my siblings and me together in our parents' home for a few days, even when we otherwise lived far away. Our gatherings were always a source of happiness—the broad smile on my mother's face at having all five of her adult children (and eventually some grandchildren) under one roof was enough to light the neighborhood. But this happiness, too, was fleeting. We would eventually go back to our own homes, jobs, and routines. Joy is not happiness, either; otherwise, those without happy circumstances would never experience joy.

Joy, like love, is intangible. You cannot touch joy, but you can similarly feel its "sweetness that pours into everything," as Helen Keller said. Joy, like love, is something experienced, and joy is inextricably linked with love. Joy, like love, is not a lonely experience. Joy is something experienced in communion and community with God and with others—our families, friends, neighbors . . . even, inexplicably, our enemies. Joy can't be sought after the way pleasures can be. Rather, joy is a gift given from a Giver who desires to give, not just occasionally, but continually—and eternally. Similarly, joy does not happen to us the way happiness can, dependent on circumstances that are sometimes in our control, but often out of our control.

We might not be happy every day; in fact, we might face suffering every day. But we can have joy every day. Running after joy is akin to holding a cup upside down. Joy is there, waiting to be given, but it doesn't enter in. Rather than running after joy the way we might seek after pleasures or happy circumstances, we must instead rest and reorient ourselves into a posture of receiving, not running. The practices I share here are meant to help us reorient ourselves, to turn our cup right side up so that joy enters, and we exclaim, in the words of the psalmist, "My cup runs over" (Psalm 23:5).

In the hours before his betrayal and death, Christ filled a cup with wine and offered it to his disciples. Before this, he spoke of love and joy to them: "These things I have spoken to you, that My joy may remain in you, and *that* your joy may be full. This is My commandment, that you love one another as I have loved you" (John 15:11–12). Christ loved us with the greatest love of all. If the joy of the Resurrection could only have happened because of Christ's sacrificial love for us on the Cross, then we will only fully experience joy through love and self-sacrifice. If we could define how to experience joy, it would be this: joy is experienced through the giving and receiving of sacrificial love.

According to church father Evagrius of Pontus, love is the "child" of joy and peace.[5] One evening I went to bed in tears over some argument with my husband. I can't even remember the argument or why I was crying, but I needed some comfort, so I picked up my Bible. My next chapter turned out to be the story of the Resurrection in the Gospel of John. I started reading, slowly, with tears in my eyes. As I read, I realized how impossible it would be for me to continue crying. Mary herself had approached the empty tomb weeping, ready to anoint Jesus's body since she had not been able to do so on the night he died. Her weeping was quickly transformed to joy when she saw her risen Savior. My tears dried quickly as I imagined this most amazing of mornings, the morning when Christ took the very worst thing that could happen—death— and robbed it of its power over us. Death, the greatest thief of joy, no longer has dominion over us because of Christ's victory.

A peace came over me, reminding me of the love I have for my husband, a love that transcended whatever petty argument we were having. Love indeed is born of joy and peace.

The call to be eternally joyful is connected to the promise and hope of eternal life. Joy is living in the hope of the Resurrection, believing in that hope with our whole hearts, without a doubt. To live in the joy born of love and peace in the face of so much that reminds us of death instead of life, our faith offers us tools we can use to help us put joy into practice. You will find seven of these spiritual practices in the chapters that follow: praying the Hours, visiting the sick, repentance, thanksgiving, hospitality, arrow prayers, and singing praise. These practices have been handed down to us over centuries of Christian tradition to help us live in the joyfulness of the Resurrection daily, despite the challenges of our everyday lives.

I am no guru, nor am I described as particularly buoyant in personality. I'm more often pensive and moody. I am a Christian who struggles, as you surely do, with challenges that steal my joy. This is why I am an "authority" on this topic, and why I have written this book. I have found that these spiritual practices have helped me keep the joy of the Resurrection, the joy of the love of God, and they have helped me experience that joy through the receiving and giving of sacrificial love.

I was born in Egypt and baptized into the Coptic Orthodox Church in my infancy. I grew up in New York and New Jersey just as the Coptic diaspora in the United States was establishing itself and expanding. I like to say that I gained my theological education through osmosis; my father is a Coptic Orthodox priest and a theologian, and so is my husband. Nonetheless, like most Coptic Orthodox Christians, I learned these spiritual practices by participation in the sacramental life of the church and the examples of the role models around me—parents, spiritual fathers, and other members of our local and extended church family, including my church family in Egypt, where I spent much time in my early adult life. An avid reader of literature and theology and an occasional seminarian, I have also been blessed to serve others in the church in different capacities, including ecumenical capacities that have allowed me to engage with and experience many different Christian traditions.

I've seen and experienced a lot of the struggle of everyday life. I don't come to the subject of joy for a moment thinking that it is easy or obvious. My professional life in international development has exposed me directly to the immense amount of pain in the world, pain that could easily lead me into despair, cynicism, and burnout. Some of that work happened in Egypt, where I would travel for months at a time and throw myself completely into the community development work I was doing. During those times, I rarely took days off. After periods of despair, cynicism, and burnout, I learned to practice joy again by taking time away from work to pray the Hours in a monastery, visit the sick with my relatives, express gratitude for the cultural differences that had frustrated me in the past, experience Middle Eastern hospitality, repeat arrow prayers on walks and train rides, and sing praise to God with the community of believers. I rediscovered my faith in these very practices, and they've taught me so much that I want to share them with you.

An early church text called *The Shepherd of Hermas* contains an injunction to "remove sorrow from yourself" and "put on joyfulness." Early Christians took this to heart in a way that needs reviving in our lives:

For every joyful man does good deeds, thinks good thoughts, and despises sorrow. But a sorrowful person always does wrong things. He does wrong first because he grieves the Holy Spirit who was given to us for joy; second, he grieves the Holy Spirit by working wrong, by not interceding and confessing to the Lord. For the intercession of a sorrowful man is never powerful enough to ascend to the altar of God. . . . Therefore, purify yourself from evil sorrow and you shall live in God. And all who cast sorrow away and put on all joyfulness shall live in God.[6]

According to *The Shepherd of Hermas*, joy for the Christian is not an option—in fact, if we do not practice it, we go so far as to grieve the Holy Spirit, and our prayers become too weak to reach God. The Church gives us the means to "put on joyfulness" so we can live in the Spirit and pray powerfully.

I am not always consistent with these seven practices, although I want to and should be. And some practices are more easily sustained than others. At the same time, this book is not meant to burden readers with more to do. The joy of the Resurrection, after all, is a grace from God that none of us have earned. There is a way of living in the gift of this incredible joy, without ever earning it but simply receiving it. These practices give us this way of living and are "means of grace," in the words of the late Bishop Samuel, one of our great religious teachers.[7] Practice doesn't make perfect. Rather, practice makes *present*. Our spiritual practices, when done consistently, with a whole heart, and with the guidance of our spiritual fathers, help us draw closer to the presence of God. They help us to live in the joy God has so generously and marvelously provided for us through his incarnation, which gave us the ability to enjoy his presence palpably.

C. S. Lewis warns us in *Surprised by Joy* not to make joy an idol, a feeling or sense to be pursued in and of itself. Joy, according to Lewis, "is distinct not only from pleasure in general but even from aesthetic pleasure. It must have the stab, the pang, the inconsolable longing."[8] That pang, that longing, is the longing we all have for God himself, for that time when we will be wholly and completely united in him. As Jesus says: "Therefore you now have sorrow; but I will see you again and your heart will rejoice, and your joy no one will take from you" (John 16:22).

God is the source of our joy, and union with Him our goal.

CHAPTER *Two*

The Joy Thieves

The world didn't give you your joy, and the world can't take it away. You can let people come into your life and destroy it, but I refused to let anyone take my joy.

—ANTHONY RAY HINTON, a few years after being released
from thirty years in prison for a wrongful conviction[9]

Sit in a high place and keep watch if you can, and you will see the thieves come, and you will discover how they come, when and from where, how many and what kind they are as they steal your clusters of grapes.

—ST. JOHN CLIMACUS, *The Ladder of Divine Ascent*

One idyllic summer evening, I sat in the backyard with my two older children. They were then ages five and two. A friend had bequeathed us a small, used swing set, and another friend had assembled it for the kids. As I sipped my coffee and watched them play, grateful for my children and generous friends, my son shouted, "Look! The tomatoes are here!"

Sure enough, some small red tomatoes were ripening in our garden. When we first moved to our home, one of our neighbors told me that our soil was especially rich, perfectly suited for a vegetable garden. I was six months pregnant with my second baby at the time, so when he said this, I nodded obligingly, vaguely referring to some future time when I might be physically and mentally capable of planting a garden and caring for it. When, after two years, he noticed that I still had not planted anything, he took matters into his own hands and planted a little vegetable garden for us himself.

My daughter slid down the slide to come see the excitement. I instructed the kids to start picking the red tomatoes while I went inside to get a basket. When I returned, my daughter happily deposited some smooth, green ones she had picked with her chubby toddler hands. I had forgotten that, at two years old, she didn't know the difference between red and green.

We laughed and put the green tomatoes on the kitchen windowsill to ripen in the sun. We later discovered that my daughter was unwittingly right about picking them green. Little critter thieves were stealing our red ones before we could get to them and enjoy them. We saw their traces in half-eaten tomatoes on the ground. My urban inexperience meant that I had no idea how to keep them out.

Joy thieves can be just like the little animals that steal tomatoes from the garden. On the outside, they can be small, cute, and furry, even comforting, and yet somehow they can still manage to steal our joy. The early church fathers called them "the passions." In this context, *passions* are not to be completely confused with our modern use of the word to describe a positive, driven desire to do something good or meaningful. Nor are they to be confused with the "passion of Christ," which is related to the Latin word for suffering and endurance. Rather, these passions are extreme versions of human behavior that lead to sin.

These passions, or *logismoi*, also called "thoughts" and sometimes called "demons,"[10] include gluttony, lust, greed, anger, envy, sloth, and vainglory. Each begins with a human thought or need that is not, in and of itself, sinful. Gluttony, for example, has its roots in hunger; lust, from normal sexual desire; anger, from a sense of injustice, and so on. It is the imbalance of these thoughts that lead to the passions, and when the passions are subdued and balance is maintained, we experience *apatheia*, which is "an abiding sense of peace and joy that comes from the full harmony of the passions."[11] *Apatheia* looks and sounds much like "apathy," but apathy is a total indifference to others, whereas *apatheia* is closer to equanimity, to being in balance and less easily moved by the passions.

Thus, the imbalance of passions can be a joy thief. Many passions, taken to an extreme, eventually manifest themselves as addictions, although they start, like fuzzy bunny rabbits, as comforts and pleasures. Recent research, for example, claims that people who habitually use curse words are happier, healthier, smarter, and perhaps more honest than those who don't.[12] These studies lead some to think that habitual cursing is a good thing. Is it a comfort of some sort— something that eases tension temporarily? Perhaps for some it is. But habitual cursing sounds to me like uncontrolled anger—no better than, say, the habitual yelling that I am prone to, which also stems from anger. Anger is a joy thief that masquerades itself through the temporary relief that might come from cursing or yelling.

The same could be said for gluttony. Many people, including me, have succumbed to "comfort eating" at one time or another, eating out of a sense of boredom or to quell other pains or anxieties. Taken to an extreme, this can result in many health problems or binge eating disorders, and so gluttony is a joy thief that disguises itself through the temporary comfort of a bowl (or two) of fettuccine alfredo.

Thus, an overindulgence in "creature comforts" can inhibit us from experiencing and practicing joy, because these pleasures are just short-term stand-ins for the joy that can only be truly found in God's love, God's comfort, and God's power. "I sometimes wonder whether all pleasures are not substitutes for Joy," C. S. Lewis writes.[13] Just like the furry bunnies stealing our tomatoes, an imbalance of the passions—the overindulgence in earthly pleasures—can steal our joy.

Even the common social injunction to college graduates to "follow their passion" when trying to find meaningful work is indirectly related to the passions the Fathers referred to. For many disappointed young people, the stress of finding or following a passion creates impatience with the boring work of persistent practice that leads to mastery, and they experience failure and false starts rather than meaningful work or a meaningful life. Cal Newport writes a compelling critique of the finding-your-passion trend in his book, *So Good They Can't Ignore You*, arguing that it is not passion but the strengthening of key skills that is an essential element for finding work you love.[14] Strengthening key skills does two things: it actually increases enjoyment because passion for your work comes with mastering your skills (not before); and it builds the "career capital" necessary to gain more resources and autonomy and lead the life you want to lead.

Thus, even Elizabeth Gilbert, author of a famous memoir about following your passion as well as "the passions," said in a podcast conversation with Krista Tippet nine years after the publication of *Eat, Pray, Love* that she prefers curiosity to passion:

I think curiosity is our friend that teaches us how to become ourselves. . . . Passion is not so constant, not so gentle, not so forgiving, and sometimes not so available. And so when we live in a world that has come to fetishize passion above all, there's a great deal of pressure around that.[15]

She goes on to explain, in terms similar to Newport's, that many people who start to pursue creative work abandon it early, surprised by how boring and tedious it can be and expecting passion instead of practice. Following our passions is not far behind being enslaved by the passions, and this can be another joy thief, causing us not only to pick our tomatoes before they ripen, but to try to eat them green.

Talking about joy in terms of spiritual practices might indeed sound boring and tedious, not joyful at all. But in the words of Tamav Lois Farag, "Spirituality is not a quick fix; it gives no instant gratification, but requires perseverance and patience."[16] It is the ongoing practice that helps us with the balance we need. The practices of joy that I describe in the coming chapters lead us away from an overreliance on creature comforts and instant gratification to a greater reliance on the experience and giving of sacrificial love. Through praying the Hours, repentance, arrow prayers, thanksgiving, and singing praise, we experience God's love, and through visiting the sick and practicing hospitality, we offer that love. As we will find, this is a virtuous cycle—giving sacrificial love often leads to receiving it, and receiving often leads to more giving.

There are other joy thieves besides the passions. Sometimes it seems as though the world is conspiring to steal our joy at every turn. Stressors—from bad traffic to natural disasters, from interpersonal conflicts to civil wars, from personal pain to trauma and even death—are all factors that can steal our joy. The way in which they can steal our joy, however, still connects to our taming of the passions. I know this firsthand.

In 2003 I was living in Washington, D.C., and while I was always a political junkie, living in D.C. dialed this obsession up several notches. My car's radio was set to National Public Radio, and every day during February and March, the war drums of the George W. Bush administration against Iraq were getting louder. Knots formed in my stomach over the implications of this. I signed petition upon petition and prayed every day that the war could be averted. I'm sure my prayers joined those of many others.

The radio dial in my car was not the only one set to NPR. My alarm clock radio was set twice: once, at 7:00 AM, to NPR, and then at 7:30 AM to the actual alarm in case the radio didn't wake me up. One morning I woke up with a start, my heart beating rapidly in fear —I thought alarms in my building were going off as bombs dropped on us. The news of war from my clock radio had entered my sleep/wake state, and I had allowed the world's news to completely bombard my psyche.

I changed my alarm setting that day to wake me up to a Gospel music station instead. Fifteen years later, it has almost universally been accepted that the Iraq war was a bad idea, with lasting and deadly consequences we are still facing today. But the knots in my stomach and the panic attack I had that morning in 2003 did nothing to stop the war, not even with my petitions and prayers. Anxiety and fear certainly stole my joy, but this was because of a passion: pride, also known as vainglory.

It was vainglory to assume that anything would be achieved by spending all that time following the news and hoping against hope that the war would be stopped. My pride led me to internalize it all into a state of anxiety. Wondering why God did not stop the war despite our prayers and petitions, despite the demonstrations and even a threatened veto by the United Nations Security Council, was of no use either. His ways are not our ways; his thoughts are not our thoughts.

The source of anxiety is often the fear that comes with feeling out of control. New parents know this feeling well; from the moment a child is born, the world becomes full of dangers we never saw before, and we now spend time worried and anxious about all the things that could happen to our children that we can't control. The news media, which thrives on disaster and scandal, feeds this out-of-control anxiety as well. Working on taming our passions reminds us of the only realm that can be in our control with God's help. Our feelings, emotions, and impulses can be balanced and the thieves of joy warded off, even if we cannot stop the wars and the struggles. The practices outlined in this book are some of the tools to help us do this.

Many external circumstances have the potential to steal our joy, but only if we leave our doors unlocked, our garden unattended. This can happen when we abandon the spiritual practices that help us experience joy. The good news is that they are there for us to begin again, one minute at a time. Joy is a state that can be entirely independent of our circumstances, sometimes even the result of going through those circumstances. In the words of Archbishop Desmond Tutu:

> Discovering more joy does not, I'm sorry to say, save us from the inevitability of hardship and heartbreak. In fact, we may cry more easily, but we will laugh more easily, too. Perhaps we are just more alive. Yet as we discover more joy, we can face suffering in a way that ennobles rather than embitters. We have hardship without becoming hard. We have heartbreak without being broken.[17]

This is how someone like Helen Keller can write about the joy of learning, the joy of discovering nature, even with the loss of her sight and hearing. This is how St. Paul can exhort his congregations to "rejoice in the Lord always" (Philippians 4:4), even while he is in chains. Thus, martyrs can face certain death with thanksgiving, and their loved ones receive news of it with joy, even while they also feel the pain of loss.

The Coptic Orthodox Church has a historic presence in Sudan, as it does in Egypt. My husband, who grew up in Sudan, went back a few years ago and visited a new church that was built in Dar al Salam, Sudan, to the anger of some Islamist groups in the area. In an attempt to destroy the church, he learned, some terrorists had given a young boy a shiny "ball" and told him to go inside the church with it and play with his friends. The little boy bounced the "ball" into the church, and it detonated.

The priest told my husband what happened when he went to find the boy's mother to tell her the terrible news of her son's death. To his surprise, when he told her the news, she began ululating. (To ululate is to joyfully cry-sing, common among women at weddings and other happy occasions in the Middle East, North Africa, and some parts of Sub-Saharan Africa.)

"My son died in the church! He is a martyr!" her ululation went. She shocked the priest with her response. "I am not worried about my son. He is in heaven now. I am worried about you. Did you get hurt?" The priest was speechless. Here was a mother who believed in the Resurrection and was practicing its joy. Nothing, not even the death of her son, could steal it.

The thief does not come except to steal, and to kill, and to destroy. I have come that they may have life, and that they may have *it* more abundantly.

(JOHN 10:10)

Practices

PRACTICE

Praying
the Hours

"In Your presence is fullness of joy."
  (PSALM 16:11)

"What is a rite?" asked the little prince.

  "That's another thing that's been too often neglected,"
said the fox. "It's the fact that one day is different from the
other days, one hour from the other hours. My hunters,
for example, have a rite. They dance with the village girls
on Thursdays. So Thursday's a wonderful day: I can take
a stroll all the way to the vineyards. If the hunters danced
whenever they chose, the days would all be just alike, and
I'd have no holiday at all."

  —ANTOINE DE SAINT EXUPÉRY, *The Little Prince* [18]

U nlike me, my mother has a naturally joyous personality.
Her smile is wide, quick, and contagious. She is well
loved by everyone she meets. When my husband was
ordained a priest—in the same congregation my father still leads
as priest—my brother warned me that I would now have to be

nice to everyone at church. "No, I don't," I replied. "Momma has that covered."

One morning, early in my childhood, I remember waking up a little earlier than usual and walking into our living room to find Mother standing alone, a small book in her hand, her eyes closed, and her face towards the East.[19] I tried in vain to get her attention. I jumped in front of her. I pulled her arm. She would not be moved. A few minutes later, she closed her small book, made the Sign of the Cross, and gave me the attention I was seeking.

My mother was praying the Morning Prayer using her *Agpeya*, and she prayed the Morning Prayer consistently, every single day. Sometimes I stood next to her, praying with my English Book of Hours as she prayed with her Arabic one. When we completed the prayer, we prayed personal prayers and then started our day. Over time, I took up the habit of praying the Morning Prayer before school, and I eventually memorized a few psalms so that on the days I did not pray at home, I could pray on the walk to school, to class in college, and on the bus or train to work when I graduated. When I was in college, I once expressed some guilt about these "transit" prayers to Fr. Antonious Makaryus, my father of confession[20] and spiritual father, feeling that my prayers on the way to where I was going were second rate compared to my mom's early morning diligence. He encouraged me to keep doing this and not allow guilt to prevent me from those prayers. Eventually, he said, those "on the way" prayers would drive me to seek more connection with God, but if I dropped them out of guilt, I would lose the habit of praying altogether. That advice was effective for me.

The Morning Prayer, meant to be prayed at dawn, commemorates the resurrection of our Lord. It is early in the morning when the two Marys find the empty tomb (see Matthew 28). So, early every morning, through the Morning Prayer, the church invites us to meet Christ in the garden as Mary Magdalene did, leaving the sorrows of the evening behind in the light of a new day to spend with him. Wiping tears away as Mary also did, we recognize him, remembering that "this *is* the day the LORD has made; we will rejoice and be glad in it" (Psalm 118:24).

The daily Morning Prayer is one practice that cultivates joy. I encourage you to try it.

Morning Prayer
—For Daily Practice

The prayer begins with a call to worship the risen Christ, asking him to help us begin anew:

"The night has passed away, we thank You, O Lord, and

ask You to keep us this day without sin and deliver us."

We then read a short passage from the Book of Ephesians, describing exactly how we might conduct ourselves this day to avoid sin:

"to walk worthy of the calling with which you

were called, with all lowliness and gentleness, with

longsuffering, bearing with one another in love,

endeavoring to keep the unity of the Spirit in the bond

of peace." (4:1–3)

With these instructions, we begin praying the Psalms of the
Morning Hour. Psalm 5 proclaims:

> "But let all those rejoice who put their trust in You; Let
> them ever shout for joy, because You defend them; Let
> those also who love Your name be joyful in You. For
> You, O LORD, will bless the righteous. With favor You will
> surround them as with a shield."

After praying the Psalms—I usually choose three out of the
Morning Prayer's nineteen—we read the Gospel of the First Hour,
John 1, which begins:

> "In the beginning was the Word, and the Word was with
> God, and the Word was God." (1:1)

This Gospel reading reminds us that the morning light is not just
the light of the sun but the light of the Son:

> "In Him was life; and the life was the light of men."
> (1:4)

The Morning Prayer reminds us to be joyful, for he has blessed
us and surrounded us with his favor—the gift of life. It is a gift
to awaken a new day and escape the dangers of the night. Psalm
13 recounts that trouble of night, the "sleep in death," and then
reminds us that our hearts "shall rejoice in Your salvation." In this
sense, every morning is a celebration, not just of Christ's resurrection but a foretelling of our own. When we arise to celebrate it in
prayer, we experience the joy of his presence, as Psalm 16 reminds
us: "In Your presence is fullness of joy."

Morning Prayer is found in the *Agpeya*, the daily office of the Coptic Orthodox Church. This is essentially a psalter, dividing the Psalms into seven prayers at seven hours of the day: Morning Prayer, at 6:00 AM; the Third Hour, at 9:00 AM; the Sixth Hour, at noon; the Ninth Hour, at 3:00 PM; the Sunset Prayer, at 5:00 PM; the Compline, at 9:00 PM, and the Midnight Hour. Each hour includes twelve or so psalms, a Gospel reading, some prayers and petitions, and a conclusion. It is a simple prayer book to follow, and it is used universally in the Coptic Orthodox Church of Alexandria by clergy, monks, and laypeople.

The *Agpeya* is, in fact, one of the Church of Alexandria's contributions to Christendom. The Psalms were regularly prayed at specific times of the day by the Jews, and the Church of Alexandria was the first to incorporate this practice into Christian worship.[21] As early as the fourth century, church fathers such as St. John Cassian were writing about this practice in Egypt, and its practice spread to other parts of the Christian world. Recently, the body of a fifth-century Egyptian Christian boy was found mummified and buried with a Coptic cross and a Book of Psalms in his hands.[22] Today, a "Liturgy of the Hours" or "Divine Office" exists in most churches with a liturgical tradition—in different forms, but with a similar structure of psalms, a Gospel reading, and some prayers and petitions.

Morning Prayer can feel challenging at first, especially to night owls like me. My mother, while a model for Morning Prayer, is also a lark who has never needed an alarm clock to wake up in the morning. I, on the other hand, am more likely to hit the snooze on my alarm clock for a few more minutes and rush through the prayer or skip it altogether—and then feel disoriented for the rest of the day. The good news for people like me is that praying the Psalms is not complicated, takes only a few minutes, does not require fancy breathing or "mindfulness" to "center" us, but instead offers words to connect us. The ancient prayers of the Psalms, sung thousands of years ago by the prophets, the disciples, and the apostles, are now sung by fellow Christians—and even non-Christians—everywhere.

Sunset Prayer

At the other end of the day comes Sunset Prayer. My father loves to recount the evenings in the southern Egyptian village where he grew up in the 1960s, when his father and grandfather would gather the family on the rooftop of their home to pray the Sunset Prayer. In these villages, rooftops are sort of like patios on the roof. Families would congregate there in the evenings to enjoy the cooler air, and sometimes even to sleep on hot Egyptian summer nights. Standing on their own rooftops, all the neighbors would join them, even the Muslim neighbors—for after all, both Muslims and Christians declare that "unless the LORD builds the house, those who build it labor in vain. Unless the LORD guards the city, the guard keeps watch in vain" (Psalm 127, NRSV), and both can pray, "In my distress I cried to the LORD, And He heard me" (Psalm 120).

Some people pray all seven hours. When my retired mother-in-law lived with us for a few months, she marked the hours of the day with her *Agpeya*. I imagine that many elderly Copts do so, although I once overheard a monk jokingly admonish a layperson, "If you pray all seven hours, what have you left us to do?" Monks and nuns order their days around these prayer hours, with some hours prayed alone and others as a monastic community. One reason, in fact, for the spread of using the Psalter in Christianity was the worldwide fascination with the desert monasticism founded in Egypt.

Praying the Hours helps us, even in the bustle of our days, to stand in God's presence and feel this "fullness of joy." The Hours are not just for ascetics, then, but even for busy, distracted laypeople, an anchor to pull us away from the storms of life into God's presence and the presence of the entire community of believers. The moment I pick up my prayer book to pray, someone else is praying the same prayer, someone else has prayed another prayer a few moments before me, and others will be praying when I stop. In this way, when I pray the Psalms, I become part of of an eternal chorus, even if it seems like I am praying alone. "For where two or three are gathered in my name, I am there among them" (Matthew 18:20).

Traci Rhoades, a Protestant writer, decided to take up praying the Hours using the *Agpeya* during a recent Lenten season. As she continued in the practice, she observed on her blog:

> It's deeply meaningful for me to think of the thousands of other believers who are praying in a similar way at the exact same time I am every day. . . . When I pick up this Prayer Book, my mind settles. A peace comes over me, and I join in.[23]

When we start praying the hours, it is as if we are stepping into a different dimension where there are countless others with us. When we make that decision to pray, we are joining them, as Rhoades describes.

I experienced this sense of an invisible community firsthand when I had my first baby. New motherhood is intimidating and often quite isolating. Days and nights blurred together as I nursed my newborn. Having the Psalter to anchor my days and nights became a comfort. While I gave my son his morning feeding at the crack of dawn, I kept my *Agpeya* by my bed and pulled it out

to pray the Morning Prayer while everyone else slept around me.
I prayed words such as these:

> The heavens declare the glory of God;
> And the firmament shows His handiwork
> (PSALM 19:1)

> God be merciful to us and bless us,
> *And* cause His face to shine upon us,
> That Your way may be known on earth, Your salvation
> among all nations. Let the peoples praise You, O God;
> Let all the peoples praise You.
> (PSALM 67:1–3)

From the Gospel, I read:

> "And the Word became flesh, and dwelt in us, and we
> beheld His glory, the glory as of the Only-Begotten of
> His Father, full of grace and truth." (JOHN 1:14)

From the Gloria, I prayed:

> "Let us praise with the angels,
> saying, 'Glory to God in the highest, peace on earth,
> and good will toward men.'"

With these prayers, I was no longer alone. The heavens were
praising God, the angels were glorifying him, and all the nations
were singing for joy at his salvation. I wasn't just nursing my child
alone with a little prayer book at the crack of dawn anymore. I was
joining the chorus of all creation.

In those trying days of first-time motherhood, praying the Hours represented God's grace for me. Rather than feeling stressed if I missed the Morning Prayer, I could pick it up again at 9:00 AM and pray the Third Hour, or at noon the Sixth Hour. The words of the Psalms soothed me.

Then, at the Sunset Hour, when anxieties overtook me, I would be reminded:

> Those who trust in the LORD *Are* like Mount Zion,
>
> *Which* cannot be moved, *but* abides forever.
>
> As the mountains surround Jerusalem,
>
> So the LORD surrounds His people
>
> From this time forth and forever.
>
> (PSALM 125:1–2)

With those words my anxieties receded to the background, as I imagined the Lord as a range of mountains surrounding my family and me, protecting us.

His Holiness Pope Shenouda III of Blessed Memory often said, "Memorize the Psalms, and the Psalms will preserve you."[24] In Arabic, *memorize* and *preserve* are homonyms: keep the Psalms and they will keep you. My experience praying the psalter has proven this for me; I hope it will for you, too. With daily repetition, eventually the words of the Psalms, Gospel readings, and ancient prayers and petitions move to my lips with ease, even when I am not standing up in prayer. Gazing out my window at some hills brings the words, "I will lift up my eyes to the hills—from whence comes my help? My help *comes* from the LORD" (Psalm 121:1–2). As I cradle my children to sleep, I whisper these words of blessing, "May the LORD answer you in the day of trouble!" (Psalm 20:1).

When Catholic writer and radio host Jennifer Fulwiler began using the Catholic Liturgy of the Hours, she initially had difficulty praying some of the psalms. Not all the verses she prayed from the Divine Office seemed to apply to her life. Some verses make me cringe too—verses like "The righteous shall rejoice when he sees the vengeance; He shall wash his feet in the blood of the wicked," (Psalm 58:10), or worse, "Happy the one who takes and dashes Your little ones against the rock!" (Psalm 137:9). Some just make me uncomfortable—verses like "You have tested my heart; You have visited *me* in the night; You have tried me and have found nothing; I have purposed that my mouth shall not transgress" (Psalm 17:3). I certainly cannot claim that God will find nothing amiss if he tests my heart, and my mouth has probably transgressed within a few minutes of writing this sentence.

The church fathers and mothers point out that the "enemies" against whom we pray for vengeance are not other human beings, but our own "passions," the thoughts and emotions that take us away from prayer and steal our joy. The enemies can also be Satan and his demons seeking to steal our joy and our salvation. Vengeance against the thoughts that prevent us from nearness to God and against the enemy that wants to steal us away from God is clearly warranted.

Over time, Fulwiler learned a key point about the Psalms and praying the Hours: "One of the first things that jumped out at me as different when I started praying the Liturgy of the Hours was that I found myself saying 'we' and 'our' more often than 'I' and 'mine.'"[25] Praying the Hours helps our prayers move beyond our personal, individual needs and into something broader. But even more than this, according to Fulwiler:

As I had yawned through the psalmist's cry of anguish, someone out there could barely utter those same words through trembling lips and tear-stung eyes. I thought of all the people praying the Hours in that state, and for the first time was conscious of our deep connectedness as we prayed in unison as part of the mystical Body of Christ. I began offering my prayers for them, which then led me to expand my prayers to anyone else in the world who was in pain at that moment. As my heart swelled to think of the great drama playing out all over the world that morning of which I was only a small part, I thought back to my words at the beginning of the office —"But this Psalm doesn't have anything to do with me!" — and realized that I had learned something critically important about prayer: It's not all about me.[25]

When we join the community of believers in this kind of prayer, we are praying *with* them, but we are also praying *for* them. We may not be violently attacked by enemies who seek to kill us at the moment, but somewhere in the world there are people who cannot leave their homes for fear of certain death. We may feel secure with our full refrigerators, but somewhere in the world— perhaps even closer than we think—someone is hungry and fears that God has forgotten them (see Psalm 13). Praying the Hours connects us to each other deeply in ways we cannot always see.

There are other psalms that make me uncomfortable, that claim righteousness I cannot claim for myself. "Vindicate me, O LORD, For I have walked in my integrity. I have also trusted in the LORD; I shall not slip. Examine me, O LORD, and prove me; Try my mind and my heart" (Psalm 26:1–2, prayed during the Third Hour). I tremble at saying these words. Can I ask God in confidence to try my heart and my mind? Have I consistently walked with integrity? Have I always trusted in the Lord? Many psalms are also prophecies, and these verses are said to be about Christ, and his righteousness, not my own. So why should I pray them on a daily basis?

Here is where the greatest miracle of prayer occurs. When praying these psalms of righteousness during the Hours, I am able to participate in the righteousness of Christ Jesus himself. I began that participation in baptism when I "put on Christ" (Galatians 3:27), and I continue in that participation daily. St. Paul exhorts us to do this every morning:

> The night is far spent, the day is at hand. Therefore let us cast off
> the works of darkness, and let us put on the armor of light. Let us
> walk properly, as in the day, not in revelry and drunkenness, not
> in lewdness and lust, not in strife and envy. But put on the Lord
> Jesus Christ, and make no provision for the flesh, to *fulfill* its lusts.
> (Romans 13:12–14)

I cannot claim a clean heart, but through Christ I can be sure that God will help me have one if I ask for it. I cannot claim to have always walked in integrity, but I can be sure that I can if Christ walks with me. I cannot claim that I have always trusted in the Lord, but I can ask the Lord to help me do that. As the words of the Psalms get imprinted in my heart through daily repetition, so the person of Christ himself does. Through Christ I can "put on the armor of light"; in fact, I can literally "put on Christ."

And then, through him and with him, I can stand in front of God and confidently ask him to "try my heart," promise that "I will behave wisely in a perfect way" (Psalm 101:2), and claim that "I have done justice and righteousness" (Psalm 119:121). In the words of St. Athanasius of Alexandria in his *Letter to Marcellinus on the Interpretation of the Psalms*:

> [T]he Lord, the true Lord of all, Who cares for all His works, did not only lay down precepts but also gave Himself as a model of how they should be carried out, for all who would to know and imitate. And therefore, before He came among us, He sketched the likeness of this perfect life for us in words, in this same book of Psalms; in order that, just as He revealed Himself in flesh to be the perfect, heavenly Man, so in the Psalms also men of good-will might see the pattern of life portrayed, and find therein the healing and correction of their own.[26]

We pray the Psalms that refer to Christ so we can pattern our lives after him, to imitate him as he has revealed himself to us. St. Athanasius exhorts us to "make the words your own," even the words that clearly refer to Christ's righteousness. Benjamin Wayman explains St. Athanasius this way: "Through praying the words of the Psalter 'as our very own,' we learn a new language that makes possible a new life in Christ. Thus, we become what we pray."[27]

Pray This Way with Your Family

The Daily Office provides a way for parents to build a prayer habit with their children so they too can continue to experience this "putting on Christ," and pattern their lives after him. In the book *This Child of Faith*, Sophfronia Scott describes how following her Episcopal church's Holy Week ritual inspired her to develop a daily prayer habit for herself and her son: "We had both experienced the bigger realm of ritual. What would happen if we brought it down to the level of the personal?"[28] Scott used *The Book of Common Prayer* as a guide, and a morning prayer podcast by an Episcopalian priest to start her off.

> Before I started going to church I wasn't a fan of prewritten prayers. I didn't understand why you couldn't just talk to God in straightforward conversation. But . . . I discovered that repeating the same prayers daily allows the words to be carved into my being, words that I can call up as comforting mantras when needed.[29]

Soon after starting her morning prayer ritual, Scott began praying the Compline with her son, eventually moving from praying it in his room before bed to praying it in their prayer and meditation space in their home, which became one of her son's favorite places to be.

Many Orthodox Christian homes have such a space, often called an "icon corner." At our home's icon corner, we have a crucifix, an icon of Christ, an icon of the Theotokos, an icon of the Resurrection, and icons of our children's name saints. Whether or not you are Orthodox, you may want to create such a space in your home.

PRACTICE

One

We also have a little table upon which are stacked several copies of *Agpeya*s for us to use. As Scott did with the *Book of Common Prayer*, my husband and I have used the *Agpeya* to instill a prayer habit for our own children, praying a protracted Morning or Third Hour prayer with them before breakfast and before they head out for school. The repeated prayers, all drawn from Scripture, not only carve themselves into our being, but help us to continue to pray even when challenges arise—packed schedules, exhaustion, boredom, or, as Fr. Peter Farrington of St. George Orthodox Ministry in the United Kingdom points out, spiritual dryness.

> The habit of praying the *Agpeya* also preserves us from abandoning
> prayer when we are facing difficulties or times of dryness. When
> we have made it a habit to pray the *Agpeya* once in the day, and
> this is the beginning of a habit, then we discover that the force of
> this habit encourages us to pray, even when we feel unwilling.[30]

I actually feel unwilling quite often. My days of first-time motherhood are over, and the freedom to pray several hours of the *Agpeya* per day are gone as well. My days are now full of caring for the needs of three young children, attending to the demands of work and home, and participating and serving at church. Force of habit brings me back to it when busyness or physical exhaustion tries to keep me from it. Missing the Morning Prayer creates a feeling akin to forgetting to brush my teeth. I will certainly get through the day, but everything will taste funny. Forgetting over a longer period of time, of course, produces a worse outcome, as St. Isaac the Syrian explains: "On that day God will not judge us about psalmody, nor for the neglect of prayer, but because by abandoning them we have opened the door to the demons."[31] Morning Prayer gives us the opportunity to spend time in God's presence, and it also empowers us to face the struggles of the day. We ask God to "protect us from every evil, every sin and every enemy," so "that we may complete this day in righteousness, purity and good order" (from the First Absolution of the Morning Hour).

In *Psalms: The Prayer Book of the Bible*, Dietrich Bonhoeffer describes some of the "demons" St. Isaac the Syrian referred to:

> The morning prayer determines the day. Squandered time of which we are ashamed, temptations to which we succumb, weakness and lack of courage in work, disorganization and lack of discipline in our thoughts and in our conversation with others, all have their own origin most often in the neglect of morning prayer. Order and distribution of our time become more firm where they originate in prayer. Temptations which accompany the working day will be conquered on the basis of the morning breakthrough to God.[32]

Squandered time, temptations, weakness, lack of courage, disorganization, lack of discipline in thoughts and conversation all can successfully steal our joy, taking our focus away from what is truly important.

And so, I still try to emulate my mother in praying the Morning Prayer, sometimes waking early to pray it on my own before the morning rush and then returning to bed. It is the Morning Hour when we thankfully rise from the slumber that mimics death and greet the new day with thanksgiving and praise. The sunlight that takes us from evening to morning reminds us that Christ our God is the True Light, and we ask him to "enlighten our minds, our hearts and our understandings" not just with

PRACTICE

One

daylight, which he gives to all creation, but with the "light of Your divine knowledge," as we ask in the First Absolution of the Morning Hour. This divine knowledge allows us to see everything through Jesus Christ our risen Lord, not simply through our own limited perspectives. At the Morning Hour, when we spend a few minutes standing in God's presence as Mary did in the Garden of the Resurrection, we can experience the fullness of joy.

PUT JOY INTO PRACTICE
Morning Prayer
—A Version to Use on Days When You Are Especially Weary

From the Prayer of Thanksgiving:

Let us give thanks to the beneficent and merciful God, the Father of our Lord, God, and Savior Jesus Christ, for He has protected, assisted, preserved, and accepted us, had compassion upon us, supported us and brought us till this hour.

From Psalm 51:

O Lord, open my lips, and my mouth shall show forth Your praise. For You do not desire sacrifice, or else I would give *it*; You do not delight in burnt offering. The sacrifices of God *are* a broken spirit, a broken and a contrite heart— these, O God, You will not despise.

From the opening prayers:

One is God; the Father of all. One is his Son who became man, died and rose from the dead on the third day, and raised us up with Him. One is the Holy Spirit, the Comforter, and the same in nature, who proceeds from the Father, and sanctifies the whole creation, teaching us to worship the Holy Trinity in one divinity, one nature. We praise Him, and we bless Him forever. Amen.

Psalm 13

How long, O Lord? Will You forget me forever? How long will You hide Your face from me? How long shall I take counsel in my soul, *Having* sorrow in my heart daily? How long will my enemy be exalted over me? Consider *and* hear me, O Lord my God; Enlighten my eyes, Lest I sleep the *sleep* of death; Lest my enemy say, "I have prevailed against him"; *Lest* those who trouble me rejoice when I am moved. But I have trusted in Your mercy; My heart shall rejoice in Your salvation. I will sing to the Lord, because He has dealt bountifully with me. Alleluia.

From the Gospel Reading:

He was in the world, and the world was made through Him, and the world did not know Him. He came to His own, and His own did not receive Him. But as many as received Him, to them He gave the right to become

children of God, even to those who believe in His name:
who were born, not of blood, nor of the will of the flesh,
nor of the will of man, but of God. And the Word became
flesh and dwelt among us, and we beheld His glory, the
glory as of the only begotten of the Father, full of grace
and truth.

From the Gospel Litanies:

When the morning hour approaches, O Christ our God
the True Light, let the senses and the thoughts of the light
shine upon us, and let us not be covered by the darkness
of pain that we may deeply praise You with David, saying:
"My eyes are awake through the night, that I may meditate
on Your word."

The Second Absolution of the Morning Hour

O Giver of light, who makes the sun shine upon the
righteous and the wicked; who created and gave light
to the world, we ask You, O Master of all, to enlighten
our minds, hearts and understanding. Grant us to please
You this present day. Protect us from every evil, every sin
and every enemy, through Jesus Christ our Lord, who is
glorified with You and with the Holy Spirit, giver of life,
consubstantial Trinity, now and forever more. Amen.

PRACTICE

Visiting
the Sick

"The kingdom of God is within you" means the joy
which the Holy Spirit plants in your hearts. For He is
the icon and the token of eternal joy which the souls
of the saints enjoy.
—St. Gregory of Nyssa[33]

In a famous story from the desert fathers and mothers, a monk
finds a cluster of grapes that had ripened before their harvest
time in the arid Egyptian desert. So he takes the grapes and
gives them to Abba Macarius, the head of the monastery. Abba
Macarius does not eat of the grapes but gives them instead to an
elderly brother who is sick. The elderly brother takes the grapes
but does not eat them, instead giving them to another brother
in the community who has not yet had anything to eat. The
cluster of grapes continues being passed around to the monks
in the community, without anyone actually partaking of it, until
it returns to Abba Macarius. In a children's song retelling this
story, when the grapes return to Abba Macarius, he gathers all

the monks together and shows them the grapes, telling them how each brother preferred to give the grapes to another brother rather than enjoy them himself, and declaring that these grapes are the cluster of love and self-sacrifice.

To truly understand the immense self-sacrifice of giving away grapes in the desert, we need to consider the time when this story is believed to have occurred. Figs, grapes, apples, dates—during the first centuries, these were perhaps the sweetest things people could eat besides honey. According to *National Geographic*, sugar did not appear in or near the Middle East until AD 600.[34] With processed sugar so plentiful in our diets today, it can be difficult to comprehend the sensation that the image of fruit conjured up for the hearers of this story. I experienced this once in a small way when I tried a diet before my wedding that involved going two weeks without sugar, including fruit. After a few days on this diet, even the sight of green sour Granny Smith apples had me salivating.

Christ speaks of grapes in the Gospel of John, right after he promises the Holy Spirit to his disciples. He says, "I am the true vine and My Father is the vinedresser. Every branch in Me that does not bear fruit He takes away; and every *branch* that bears fruit He prunes, that it may bear more fruit" (John 15:1–2). Galatians 5:22–23 says that the fruit of the Spirit is "love, joy, peace, longsuffering, kindness, goodness, faithfulness, gentleness, self-control." Joy appears as the second fruit, right after love, which is "the greatest of these" (1 Corinthians 13:13). The fruit of the Spirit conjures the sweetest food available at the time: fruit. This is the sweetness we crave, the sweetness we are honestly starving for. It is the fruit that is missing from our sugar-laden, materialistic culture.

In the same way the grapes in the story of Abba Macarius were distributed, joy as a fruit of the Spirit is not only something we should seek to experience for ourselves; it is a gift to be given to others who are craving it. With the Holy Spirit dwelling within us as Christ promised, we will not only feel joy in our hearts because of the grace within, but we will be joy to others, to everyone we encounter. The greatest mystery is that in being joy to others, we ourselves feel joy. In a glorious circle, we get to taste of the very same fruit we bear for others.

Spreading this sweetness is our offering to the world as Christians. In his commentary on the Coptic Orthodox Rite of Palm Sunday, His Grace Bishop Mettaous offers a beautiful analogy for how a Christian should be like a palm tree and its fruits. A palm tree, he writes, "gives sweet fruits: the virtues of a believer should be sweet to whoever gets in contact or deals with him." Palm trees have deep, strong roots that cannot be shaken. "So should the believer be, strong in his love to God, rooted in the grace of the Holy Spirit." A palm tree does not have many branches to climb the way other trees do, and thus animals cannot climb them to eat their fruit, so believers should not allow thieves to steal their joy. At the same time, palm trees are forgiving: "If anyone throws a rock on a palm tree, it will give back some of its sweet dates, and so a Christian person should be forgiving those insulting or humiliating them." No aspect of a palm tree is useless. Its stalks and stems are used for roofing, its leaves for basket weaving, its dates for eating. Believers should similarly be completely useful to all those around them, offering themselves the way the palm tree offers itself. The branches of fruit-bearing trees hang downward from the weight of the fruit, whereas "the trees that are without fruits have branches heading above, in pride and haughtiness. So is a believer who bears the fruits of the Spirit, he is always humble, meek and gentle."[35]

I love the contrast between a tree with no fruit, its branches high and haughty, and a palm tree heavy with fruit and therefore hanging downward, humbly offering its fruit to those who want it, even by dropping more fruit, offering sweetness to an enemy who might throw a rock at it. This is the sweetness we offer to the world as Christians—joy offered to others in humility and love. And if we are diligent in our prayers, rooted in our faith and our relationship with God, we will not be shaken, no matter how many rocks are thrown at us or how many dates are collected from us. In this act of self-sacrifice, we'll be even more joyful, because when the fruit is collected, we'll be able to bear more fruit.

"Unfortunately," Fr. Tadros Malaty writes in *An Invitation to the Happy Life*, "many people's understanding of their mission to pour out joy unto others is merely through superficial human courtesies, through an outward smile, and humor! Our Lord Jesus Christ has poured His joy within us through the blood of His Cross, and His true practical love. Thus, we can only pour joy onto others through His Spirit and through our daily cross."[36] Matthew 25 explains what this daily cross might be.

The Parable of the Talents begins with the story of three servants, each given by their master a certain number of talents to use. One receives five talents, and by putting the money to work increases them to ten; one receives two, and similarly increases them to four, but one receives one talent, and buries it rather than increasing it as the other two servants did. The parable ends with the invitation to those who increased their talents to "enter into the joy of your lord." It would seem at face value that the "joy of the Lord" is given to wise investors of money. But immediately following this parable is this passage:

"When the Son of Man comes in His glory He will set the sheep on His right hand, but the goats on the left. Then the King will say to those on His right hand, 'Come, you blessed of My Father, inherit the kingdom prepared for you from the foundation of the world: for I was hungry and you gave Me food; I was thirsty and you gave Me drink; I was a stranger and you took Me in; I *was* naked and you clothed Me; I was sick and you visited Me; I was in prison and you came to Me.' Then the righteous will answer Him, saying, 'Lord, when did we see You hungry and feed *You*, or thirsty and give You drink? When did we see You a stranger and take *You* in, or naked and clothe *You?* Or when did we see You sick, or in prison, and come to You?' And the King will answer and say to them, 'Assuredly, I say to you, inasmuch as you did *it* to one of the least of these My brethren, you did *it* to Me.'"

(MATTHEW 25:31–40)

In the Parable of the Talents, those "to whom much has been given" have been given many opportunities. What if those opportunities are chances to "pour themselves out" by pouring joy into others through serving the hungry, thirsty, naked, sick, and imprisoned? What if, when given five opportunities to "pour ourselves out" by serving others, our service leads to five more opportunities to do so? What if, in serving five people, those five people are then able to "pour themselves out" and serve five more people?

Social science has certainly proven that people are often happier when they serve others than when they pursue personal pleasure-seeking activities. A recent and often-cited study on adolescents published by the National Academy of Science in 2014 showed that adolescents participating in unselfish activities (defined as activities with "meaning and purpose") were less likely to suffer depression than those who engaged in hedonistic activities.[37] Putting joy into practice in this regard is the ultimate paradox—to be joyful, one must pour oneself out into the most "joyless" of situations: hunger, thirst, sickness, and imprisonment.

I find the thought of this a bit overwhelming at times, mainly because the world I inhabit is that of raising young children in the suburbs, physically far from the encounter with many of society's ills. Occasional donations to charities and food pantries aside, the only hungry and thirsty I encounter every day are my own children in the morning, clamoring for breakfast. There is, however, one practice that we as a family have taken up that has brought us joy: visiting the sick.

Sickness is an inescapable reality of life, whether you live in Calcutta or middle-class suburban America. Visiting those with ongoing illnesses or terminal diseases such as cancer or multiple sclerosis may seem like the most joyless of services. Unlike hunger, which can be met with food or thirst that can be sated with drink, visiting the sick does not often bring healing of the physical nature (although the spirit and body are linked). It brings a different kind of healing. Visiting the sick helps heal the loneliness and isolation sickness often brings about. It helps reduce the sense of hopelessness and despair that people who are chronically ill often feel. My friend Mirette, a physician's assistant at a hospital, once shared this observation after a recent shift: "Today I saw my patient light up and become a completely different person because of her visitors." That inspired her to do her own visitations more often.

Several years ago my husband began a custom with our family to go out and visit the sick of our congregation every Christmas and Easter. Some are homebound or hospital-bound, unable to make it to church to celebrate the feast, and thus we bring the feast to them. Others are heartsick, often finding it difficult to celebrate the feast after the recent loss of a loved one. It's a custom my husband had practiced when he was living in Egypt, before we were married and before he was ordained a priest. We carried it into our marriage and family life not so much by planning and discussion, but because it was his default, whereas I was more accustomed to spending the feasts at home with my family. Despite being initially resistant to these visits, I've now started to cherish them, as they are some of the few chances our whole family gets to serve God together. These visits to Christ himself now make sense to me—we are celebrating him, after all, on these feasts, so shouldn't we be visiting with him and his brethren? I cherish them because they bring joy to the people we visit—we can see it on their faces, especially with our children filling often empty, lonely spaces with childish laughter and play.

My children are not always thrilled to spend their feast days in hospitals and nursing homes when they could be spending them with their cousins and friends. To make the tradition real for them, I often recount a famous story of Abba Bishoy (also spelled Pishoy), a desert father who is my husband's name saint. Once, Abba Bishoy was promised by God that he would see Jesus Christ himself on the desert mountain of Scetis. So he told all the monks with him, and on the appointed day, the monks rushed to climb up the mountain to see Christ. At the foot of the mountain was an elderly man, who kept asking people to help him up the mountain. The monks rushed past, no one wanting to be delayed by an old man when the Lord Jesus himself was going to appear at the top of the mountain. Abba Bishoy, however, stopped to help the man and carried him on his shoulders. As he walked up the mountain, he felt the man getting lighter and lighter. Eventually when he reached the top, he looked up and saw that he was carrying Christ himself on his shoulders. The rest of the monks had seen him too—and passed him by.[38] Thus, in many Coptic Orthodox churches, the icon of Abba Bishoy portrays him carrying Christ on his shoulders. When I share this story with my children, we all realize that we don't want to be the ones to miss out on seeing Jesus Christ himself on the feast—and there are many more days to spend with our family and friends.

Visiting the sick requires us to make some space in our lives, away from activity and productivity to something that frankly we often want to avoid because we are uncomfortable with it. Sometimes I fear those quiet or awkward moments when there might not be much to say. Sometimes there are sights and smells that are difficult to bear. Sometimes the people we visit are angry, hurt, or in extreme pain, and our time together is far from pleasant. This giving of time, however inconvenient or difficult, is part of the pouring out of ourselves that gives joy to others. The moments of connection, of relationships that can be built when we pay a visit and have a conversation, are where we experience joy as well.

Visiting the sick brings comfort, and when we do it, we participate in the work of the Holy Spirit, "the Comforter, who is everywhere and fills all things," as the ancient prayer goes. St. Didymus the Blind, a Coptic saint from the fourth century, wrote:

> The Lord called the Holy Spirit whom He sent "the Comforter"
>
> because of its function. For He is not only giving comfort to those
>
> who deserve it and saves them from all anguish and distress of the

PRACTICE *Two*

soul, but also in the meantime he grants them assured joy that never dissolves. Thus resides in their hearts eternal joy where the Holy Spirit dwells.[39]

After the birth of my first child, I myself experienced the loneliness and anxiety of new motherhood as a kind of "anguish and distress of the soul." A friend named Annie offered to help me with a move to a new apartment when my baby was only three weeks old. At the time, she was more of an acquaintance, but my soul was crying out for comfort, and it was almost impossible to unpack boxes with a newborn who wanted to nurse all day, so I gratefully accepted. Her visitations were a generous gift that did wonders for my soul, and they planted the seeds of an ongoing friendship.

My sister Martha once wrote a blog post about her experience of being sick and being visited after she broke her hip in a gym accident. She shares that "other than the less-than-wise words of a few people, this has been a beautiful experience." Many of us believe, as she once did, that visitors would be tiring and someone who is sick wants rest and quiet. For Martha, however, it was the opposite. "The love I was given made despair seem like a silly afterthought. . . . When everyone around me was just happy that I was alive and healing, it brought me back to reality."[40]

The confining space of a hospital room can easily cause one to lose perspective; visitors can help a patient feel like a person again, helping him or her to regain perspective beyond medical treatment. I'm sure many others who have been sick and have received visitors can attest to the sense of joy that comes from feeling loved, from not being forgotten at a time of need, from seeing light in a time of darkness, both physically and spiritually.

Martha mentioned the "less-than-wise words" she received during some visitations. These included questions about the details of her accident that were meant mostly to satisfy the visitor's curiosity, even though it caused her to relive a very painful situation. They were also often well-intentioned lectures about weightlifting and fitness that she, an experienced personal fitness trainer at an elite gym, did not need to hear. It is possible that visiting a sick person could result in discomfort rather than comfort and despair rather than joy.

Dr. Albert Rossi talks about this in detail in his podcast, *Becoming a Healing Presence*, on Ancient Faith Radio, especially during his first episode when he describes the visits seminarians paid to his late wife during the last months of her life when she was suffering from metastasized bone cancer. She would ask him to send over a seminarian to have lunch with her, and often that visit would lift her spirits. But sometimes it didn't:

On occasion, I would ask the seminarian to come. He would come. Supper time I would say to my wife, "How was lunch, honey?" She would say, "Al, please don't ever let that seminarian enter my screen door again. I'm too sick to have a seminarian come here and play priest." That was like her definition. Someone came from the seminary and "played priest," and she was too sick to tolerate that. So, of course, I would say, "Honey, I will make sure that that person doesn't come back."

The scene would have been like this, because I've seen it played out. A seminarian would come in, perfunctorily question, "How are you doing?" And even before the full answer would be out, the seminarian would launch into a mini lecturette, a little sermonette. Then say, "I hope that you're feeling better. I have to go now. Bye," and walk out the door. The screen door would slam behind him.

He wouldn't walk out light of foot. And almost in a sense chalk it off as, "Yes, I visited the sick. Next thing to do." He had no idea that the sick person that he visited was lessened, was diminished by his visit.[41]

The common thread running through these experiences is that visiting the sick is not about finding the right words to say, giving a sermon, or asking intrusive questions. A visit to the sick that brings the joy of the Holy Spirit is a visit that provides giving, listening, and connection. Bring bright flowers, a gift, a meal, or your hands and feet to serve when needed or asked. Bring listening ears and the ability to be silent when necessary. Bring a smile, a song to sing, or a story to tell. Bring a piece of art or craft you have made—or bring supplies to create something together. *Be* joy, and expect to experience the joy of visiting Christ himself. Christ certainly needs no sermons from us.

Visits to the sick can sometimes very literally relieve pain. I once visited a friend at the hospital whose terminally ill father had been admitted. Both she and her father were artistic, and so I brought her an adult coloring book with inspirational Bible verses and some paintbrush markers to help her pass the time with him there. While we sat together, we decided to do some coloring to try out the new markers. Her father was harnessed with too many tubes in his arms to join in, but his eyes brightened with interest as he watched us color next to him. We did not need to say much, but we took his mind off his pain for a few minutes as he took interest in the art and color unfolding beside him.

Music and stories help relieve suffering. My oldest child, when he's home sick from school, will often ask me to tell him a story to get his mind off his pain. Studies have shown that children who listen to music or audiobooks soon after surgery register less pain than those who listen only to silence.[42] When visiting a sick child, bring a storybook or two to read together, or a song to sing together. These all relieve pain with the medicine of connection.

Experiencing joy while serving is indeed the surprising effect of serving. An elderly member of my church was living indefinitely in a rehabilitation center, and while her family visited her on a regular basis, my husband asked a few other congregation members to also visit her and keep her company. One of those congregation members was a young friend undergoing her own difficult life challenges, but she made time every two weeks or so to visit this elderly woman. I joined her once on a visit and, after ignoring the smell of urine-soaked sheets and rooms not yet cleaned, I witnessed, not just a change in the demeanor of the elderly woman, but a change in my friend's demeanor as well. She rejoiced at meeting with the elderly woman. Over time they had developed a rapport, joking with each other as if they had known each other their whole lives despite only meeting each other less than a year before. The elderly woman was thirsty and grateful for the company; the younger woman forgot, for a time, her own problems as she built companionship with the elderly one. I left that visit realizing that the joy of visiting grew as their friendship grew. What externally looked like an act of self-sacrifice was actually an act of mutual giving: a mutual exchange of joy.

My husband and I recently met Layla, a young woman from Syria who had married a member of our church congregation and emigrated to the US. While living in Syria during the civil war and the rise of the so-called "Islamic State of Iraq and Syria" (ISIS), she worked in a hospital run by nuns. This hospital would regularly receive threats from ISIS for providing medical care for injured people ISIS wanted dead. Layla showed us a photograph she took with her phone of a rocket that landed in the baby nursery of that hospital. Despite the threats and rocket attacks, the hospital staff and volunteers continued working and caring for the sick and injured. Perhaps the most shocking thing Layla shared, however, was this: "I want to go back to Syria. I miss serving there." Layla, in the security of her new home in the US, misses her days serving the sick in war-torn Syria because she was, against all odds, practicing joy, and in the midst of rocket fire and shrapnel, it tasted sweet.

Not every visitation to a sick person is pleasant or even initially welcomed. Visitations should always be with the permission of the person or family being visited, but even these visits are not always treated with welcome. Sometimes people who are physically sick, or heartsick, lash out in anger. Speaking out of emotional or physical pain, they might complain about their situation, about being neglected, or blame God for their circumstances. In these cases, it is wisest to whisper a silent prayer for God's help and offer a listening ear without any tired platitudes. If the patient is open, perhaps reading a psalm together (such as Psalm 13) would be helpful. But if not, listening with empathy is best. Their complaints might be justified, and blaming God for allowing their situation understandable. God does not need us to defend him, and what he allows is a mystery to all of us. Sometimes, a joyful encounter includes some pain.

Visits like these can be emotionally draining rather than rewarding. We might not hear a word of thanks or get a smile for our troubles, especially if the visitation is with a family member, friend, or relative who expects and needs more of it. Some individuals might not remember previous visits, or even our names. We might not get to sing our song or read our story or do whatever else we had on our agenda for the visit, even though these might have been welcomed eagerly by others.

Where do we draw our joy from if the visitation itself is so thankless? The key to having more joy is *being* joy itself, and the way *to be* joy is to be filled with the Spirit, not with our own pride or power. When we are filled with the Spirit, we will be able to pour ourselves out in self-sacrifice. During the litanies of the Third Hour in the *Agpeya*, we ask for this filling up of the Holy Spirit daily: "O Heavenly King, the Spirit of Truth, the Comforter, who is everywhere and fills all things, treasury of goodness and giver of Life, we ask you to graciously come and dwell within us." And in the Divine Liturgy of St. Basil, we ask the Father to "fill our hearts with joy and gladness, that we, having sufficiency, may abound in every good deed."

When we serve others, freely giving from the joy and gladness inside us, there in our encounter, despite what it may seem like externally, we will also see God. We will see his image even in the most sickly or angry person. And like St. Bishoy, we won't pass him by.

I slept and I dreamed that life is all joy. I woke and I saw that life is all service. I served and I saw that service is joy. (KHALIL GIBRAN)

PUT JOY INTO PRACTICE

Visiting the sick takes time, but not as much time as we imagine. Those who need our visitation are often closer than we think. Some are homebound in our own neighborhoods. Some are at nearby rehabilitation centers, nursing homes, or hospitals. Some are only sick for a short time, such as those with an injury that will take a few weeks to heal, while others have chronic illnesses and spend much time in and out of medical care. All of those need the joy of a visitation, and all of us need to be joy for them.

Take a moment now to think of someone sick—or heartsick— that you can visit and serve. Perhaps you have a relative with a chronic illness or a friend who has experienced loss. Your neighbors may be adjusting to a newborn and could use a helping hand. If you cannot think of anyone, ask around. Clergy usually know who in your religious community might be in need of a visit.

Perhaps you have a friend who is part of the "sandwich generation," taking care of an elderly parent while also caring for children. Offer that friend a few hours off to rest every so often or do something they want to do while you spend that time with their family. If possible, consider offering those few hours on a regular basis, perhaps once a month.

Perhaps you are that sick person who needs a visit. It does take courage to share our vulnerability with others, especially if we have been accustomed to being the givers. When we feel this way, it is important to remember that if we don't seek assistance, we deny others the opportunity and blessing to help—we deny others the opportunity to experience joy. When you share a need for help, you are actually being a joy-giver.

Earlier in this chapter I mentioned my friend Annie, who helped me move into my new apartment after I had my first child. A few years later I shared with her how important that assistance was for me, how much I needed her companionship in addition to her moving help. She shared with me that she had just as much need for companionship, having also just moved to a new state and having been in her first few years of marriage. She looked forward to our visits as much as I looked forward to her arrival. In asking for help, I unwittingly helped her. Had I not shared my vulnerability with her, she and I would not have had the opportunity to share joy.

•

PRACTICE

The Joy
of Repentance

[L]ike a nursing mother whose face is full of joy
for her child . . . even if he is full of all kinds of
uncleanness, she does not turn away from that
bad smell and excrement but takes pity on him
and lifts him up and presses him to her breast, her
face full of joy, and everything about him is sweet
to her. If, then, this created person has pity for her
child, how much greater is the love of the creator,
our Lord Jesus Christ, for us!
— ABBA MACARIUS [43]

> Restore to me the joy of Your salvation,
> And uphold me *by Your* generous Spirit.
> *Then* I will teach transgressors your ways,
> And sinners shall be converted to You.
> PSALM 51:12–13

have to admit, it's not unusual for me to spend Sunday morning yelling at my kids to get dressed and ready for church. One such morning, even before I had my third child, involved trying to find my daughter's sparkly pink shoes while my older son played with his trains instead of getting dressed. I had given my daughter dry Cheerios to eat while I threatened to take the toy train from my son. I took him to his room, and as my mother-in-law helped him get dressed, my daughter walked in with a cake still in its plastic container. She asked her grandmother to cut her a piece, clearly having given up on Mom feeding her anything good, but then she decided she didn't actually like the cake and dropped her piece on the floor. Fearing an ant infestation, I quickly started to clean up the mess and asked my son to take the rest of the cake to the kitchen, only for him to drop the entire thing on his way through the hallway. "We'll never get to church on time!" I yelled.

We eventually made it to church that morning, albeit an hour and a half late, and I had already yelled at my kids several times. I could have excused myself that day as well as many times after, especially when my mother-in-law went back to Egypt and I had three kids to get ready while my husband was already at church starting the liturgy. But my challenges that morning were simply kids being kids, and after buckling them into their seat belts, I did the only right thing to do: I apologized for losing my patience and yelling at them. When I repented of my wrongdoing and reconciled with my children, I felt joy.

Repentance is not commonly a part of our contemporary discourse, and it's rarely associated with joy. Denial and defensiveness are more common reactions when one is accused of or even realizes wrongdoing. Repentance requires humility, and it conjures tears, sorrow, grief for wrongs done, sometimes even an expectation of retribution. The Parable of the Pharisee and the Publican (see Luke 18:9–14) gives us the image of the publican standing at the back of the temple, beating on his chest in recognition of his sins. Similarly, the Gospels give us the image of the sinful woman who washes Jesus's feet with her tears and dries them with her hair (see Luke 7:38). These are the images we most often see when we think of repentance, and the feelings of humiliation and sadness are emotions I certainly would rather avoid.

The second and third Sundays of the Lenten Lectionary give us two more repentance stories that lead us down a different path, a path with fewer tears and more joy. On the second Sunday we read the Parable of the Prodigal Son, and on the third Sunday we read the story of the Woman at the Well. Both Gospel readings take us from tears of sorrow to something different: the joy of repentance. The story of the Samaritan woman further gives us a way to practice the joy of repentance when she shares these words with her fellow Samaritans: "Come see a Man who told me all things that I ever did" (John 4:29).

First, the parable. While it is most well known as the Parable of the Prodigal Son, I've also heard it described as the Parable of the Loving Father. However, I'd like to call it the "Parable of the Party in Heaven," because that's what repentance does. The prodigal's story is well known: the younger son, tired of working the fields in his father's house, asks for his inheritance early so he could go make his fortune in the city. It's an odd and insulting request to a parent. I can't imagine how I would react if one of my children asked me for his or her portion of their inheritance, as if to say, "Not only do I want to leave you and seek my own way, but I want all the money I will get from you when you die." In other words, "I want to completely end my relationship with you." I've lost my temper at far smaller infractions.

Yet the loving father acquiesces and gives his son his inheritance. The son takes the money and goes on to live a profligate life until his money runs out and he is left in the most humiliating of circumstances—feeding swine, so hungry he could eat their leftovers. To a Jewish audience aware of swine being "unclean" animals (see Deuteronomy 14:8), this is lower than rock bottom.

It's at this point of desperation that the son remembers how much he missed his father's house—even as a servant there, he would eat better than he was eating with the pigs. He realizes how badly he insulted his father and resolves to go back in repentance, asking not to be treated like a son (for he has already severed his relationship with him as his son), but to be treated as a hired worker.

But the son underestimated his father's love. According to the law, the request he made to his father should have been met with a stoning, not with a pile of cash (see Matthew 15:4). Perhaps the fact that his father had not sent him into judgment at his first request gave the prodigal son the confidence that he would not be turned away, that he might be accepted at least as a servant upon his return. He knew he had a loving father. True to his father's character, the father, when he saw his son coming down the road from afar, did not even respond to the words his son had rehearsed. Instead, in the words of St. Athanasius of Alexandria, the father

> . . . neither receives him as a hired servant, nor does he look upon
> him as a stranger. But he kisses him as a son, brings him back to
> life as from the dead, counts him worthy of the divine feast, and
> gives him his former and precious robe. So that, on this account,
> there is singing and gladness in the paternal home. For this is the
> work of the Father's lovingkindness and goodness, that not only

should He make him alive from the dead, but that He should render His grace illustrious through the Spirit.[44]

There is a party in heaven and on earth. The prodigal's repentance and the love of the father bring him from death to life, from shame to glory, from estrangement to acceptance, from the image of sin to the image of Christ himself. St. Athanasius explains that the Parable of the Prodigal Son is the story of all humanity, and the gifts he is given upon his return are the gifts we have been given through the incarnation, death, and resurrection of Christ when we also return and repent. Repentance leads to the joy of the Resurrection.

When I first drafted these words, my eyes welled up in tears for the first time, despite having read and heard this parable so many times before. Perhaps it's because I am meditating on this story for the first time as a parent, imagining my child willfully gone from me and me sitting by the window, waiting for him to come back. I cannot imagine the overwhelming joy I would feel on his or her return, something indeed akin to a party in heaven. Tears of waiting and weeping would give way to tears of joy, and these tears of joy are one aspect of the joy of repentance.

The woman at the well shows us another side of that joy. A party only gets better when more people are invited, and that's what the Samaritan woman does after she meets Jesus.

The story in the Gospels is not a parable, but a face-to-face encounter between a sinful woman and our Lord Jesus Christ. This encounter completes our understanding of repentance and its joy. It begins by Christ himself feeling thirsty and going to Jacob's Well to drink at the sixth hour. Many Bible commentators have noted the similarity between Christ's meeting with the Samaritan Woman and the hour when he would be crucified later. The sixth hour seems to be the hour of salvation, of reconciliation.

One clue we have of the sinful life of the Samaritan woman is the hour she goes to draw water from the well. Fr. Tadros Malaty points out that while most of the women would draw water earlier in the day to avoid the heat, she goes at midday to avoid other people, to avoid their stares and their judgment.[45]

On that particular day she finds the Son of God, thirsty and asking her for a drink of water. She can tell he is a Jew and asks why he would ask her, a Samaritan, to draw water for him. They continue their conversation, with the thirsty Jesus offering the water-drawing woman living water. Unlike the prodigal son meeting his father, this encounter is a conversation. The Samaritan woman has not hit rock bottom yet, but her plea for living water, so she would not need to return to the well again every day, shows she is getting close.

It is Jesus who points out her sin by asking her to go get her husband. She replies truthfully, "I have no husband," and the Lord commends her for her honesty, knowing she has had five husbands and is living with a man she is not married to—and telling her he knows this. The Gospels are not memoirs, so we can only imagine what went on in the Samaritan woman's mind. Perhaps she felt discomfort at Christ's revelation of her past, or perhaps she finally felt at ease with someone who recognized her completely. I would imagine she experienced both of these emotions.

All we know from the Gospels is that when the encounter with Christ is over, the Samaritan woman has completely changed. Rather than hide from the townspeople by drawing her water at high noon, she runs to them, excitedly telling them about the man "who told me all things that I ever did." Her repentance may not have been marked by the tears of the publican, but she has otherwise done a complete *metanoia*—a return to God, the true meaning of repentance. The fathers even point out that leaving behind her water pot signified leaving behind her old life of sin and heading into a new life of joy and sharing. "And having received Christ the Lord into her heart," St. Augustine of Hippo writes, "What could she do but now leave her water pot, and run to preach the gospel? She cast out lust, and hastened to proclaim the truth."[46]

The story of the woman at the well reveals to us that repentance is not just about weeping and feeling shame for our sins. True and complete repentance is a response to love, and as a response to love, repentance is joy. As Origen of Alexandria points out:

Her confession is not the result of painful reprimand or confronting her with her shameful self. It is the result of His love. This arouses her conscience and reveals to her the reality of the Lord. Consequently, she becomes trustful and admits the truth about her personal life as she realizes that He can heal her wounds and restore her spiritual health.[47]

In his commentary on this portion of the Gospel of John, Origen portrays the Samaritan woman's repentance as all joy—joy for her, joy for the city, and joy for Christ himself. And her joyous redemption foretells the joy of the Resurrection:

She informed everyone in the streets that she had found the treasure she has been looking for, and that she has found the Source of her inner joy. . . . Here is a woman who proclaims the Messiah to the Samaritans. At the end of the gospels there is also another woman who is the first one to see Him and who informs the disciples about the Resurrection of the Lord Jesus Christ (John 20:18). This is all what this Samaritan woman had done. . . .

The Lord Jesus Christ seizes every chance to lift the minds and hearts of the disciples to matters beyond time and to the heavens themselves. He reveals to them the extent of His joy that arises from the redemption of souls.[48]

The joy of repentance demonstrated in the parable of the Prodigal Son is the joy of the heavens when someone turns from his sins and goes back to God. The joy of repentance in the story of the Samaritan woman is the joy experienced by the Samaritan woman herself, having left behind her old life and transformed it into something new. She cast away her old water pot so she could instead be filled with living water, and one of the marks of her repentance was the courage she had to share her encounter with the entire community.

St. John Chrysostom writes of this courage in Homily 8 of *On Repentance and Almsgiving*:

> Be ashamed when you sin. Do not be ashamed when you repent.
> . . . These are two things: sin and repentance. Sin is a wound; repentance is a medicine. Just as there are for the body wounds and medicines, so for the soul are sins and repentance. However, sin has the shame and repentance possesses the courage.[49]

The Samaritan woman's repentance showed courage. The shame that drove her to draw water at the sixth hour converted to the courage that drove her to tell all of Samaria about the man "who told me all things that I ever did."

The Samaritan woman's repentance led to her *metanoia* and the *metanoia* of all of Samaria. The Greek word *metanoia*, which we translate to mean repentance, actually means "a complete turning around." Samaria itself turned around on the witness of the woman at the well, after first rejecting Christ's visitation (see Luke 9:53). Repentance is not just about tears but about transformation—from shame to courage, from hearts of stone to hearts of compassion, from defeat to victory, from sorrow to joy. His Holiness Pope Shenouda writes:

> Repentance is joy in heaven and on earth. It is written, "There will
> be joy in heaven over one sinner who repents" (Luke 15:7,10). So
> if you wish to make heaven joyous, repent. It is joy on earth also:
> joy for the penitent, the pastor, and all the Church. Repentance
> is joy, as it is an invitation to liberty for the captives (Isaiah 61:1).
> It is joy for the freedom from slavery of Satan and sin, joy in the
> new pure life, and joy in forgiveness. It is a joy, for repentance is
> the life of victory and the song of the victorious.[50]

The victorious song of the Samaritan woman is read in the Coptic Orthodox church's lectionary three times—during the Great Lent, during the Holy Fifty Days, and during the Kneeling Prayer at Pentecost. The Samaritan woman is an emblem of the joy of repentance, the joy of the Resurrection, and the joy of receiving the Holy Spirit.

This brings us back to the Holy Spirit, whose presence in us is shown by bearing fruit, including joy. Thus, the joy of repentance is not just an internal feeling, but one demonstrated by its fruit, the same fruit the Samaritan woman bore by sharing her encounter with Christ to others so they might also taste the sweetness of the living water. The analogy of the palm tree we talked about in the previous chapter fits well again here, because it will not stand tall nor bear any fruit without being watered by the living water.

From Byzantine hagiography, we learn that the Samaritan woman gains the name Photini when she is baptized on the day of Pentecost, along with her five sisters and two sons. Her witness in the Gospels as well as her witness in Christian tradition gains her the title "Equal to the Apostles," and she eventually receives the crown of martyrdom under Emperor Nero—but not before converting hundreds of people to Christianity.[51] The joy of her repentance led to the redemption of many souls—and more joy to her Savior, who granted her his living water.

Repentance makes room for joy within us, room that was previously filled with sin, shame, and fear. When we repent by turning our lives around like the prodigal son and the Samaritan woman, we experience its joy, and it is contagious. The heavens rejoice. The church rejoices. We cannot help sharing that joy with others, so they too might encounter Christ. Putting joy into practice means practicing repentance, even on a daily basis. In the *Agpeya*, the introductory prayer for every hour includes praying Psalm 51, David's repentance prayer. It is said that this psalm was written after the prophet Nathan called out King David for sending Uriah to his death and marrying Bathsheba. In it is a verse that could have been written about the Samaritan woman: "Restore to me the joy of Your salvation, and uphold me *by Your* generous Spirit. *Then* I will teach transgressors Your ways, and sinners shall be converted to you."

The result of repentance is the joy of salvation, the renewal of the Holy Spirit, and the courage to "teach transgressors" God's ways, in the way the Samaritan woman did. In some church traditions, "teaching transgressors" has been interpreted to mean sharing personal testimonies of lives changed so that others, upon hearing these repentance stories, might also return to God. I've heard many of these personal testimonies, and they are truly inspiring and compelling, but they can divert the listener's attention to the life of the person telling it, the before-and-after story, rather than to Christ, the one who brought about the change.

The Samaritan woman's method was different. She did not go around Samaria telling people, "I used to be a fornicator, but now I am completely changed!" She went around telling people, "I met this man! He told me everything I have ever done! You should meet him too!" The result was that those in Samaria that believed returned and told her, "Now we believe, not because of what you said, for we ourselves have heard *Him*" (John 4:42). In other words, she told of her repentance not by repeating her past sins but by leading people to the Lord himself.

This is how to practice the joy of repentance. First, to truly repent, which means a *metanoia*, a complete return to God, no longer following sin but following Christ. This kind of repentance is a recognition of a life facing the wrong direction, walking down the wrong path, and turning around to follow the right path. This is the repentance that starts the "party in heaven."

Some of us can mark the moment we decided to reorient our lives toward God. I remember this happening to me at age twelve. Despite my having spent my whole life in the church, Christianity was still an external activity for me, until finally one evening I could no longer live with the disparity between my heart, which was full of dishonesty and anger, and my external actions at church, which were all holiness. There were probably many factors that brought me to that point, not the least the prayers of my parents, my church family, and my father of confession. I might have also been helped along by some Christian novels my father regularly gave me that usually featured characters going through a similar conversion—at the time I was reading *East of Outback* from Sandy Dengler's *Australian Destiny* series. I don't remember much about the book now, but I do remember finishing it, kneeling in prayer and tears, and then later confessing to my mother some things I had been dishonest with her about. I remember the relief I felt; life for me began anew after that *metanoia*.

Soon enough I learned that repentance doesn't end with that one decision, because if it did, I would have soon despaired. The life of a Christian is the life of one who falls and gets up, falls and gets up, as many fathers have noted, a life of continual *metanoia*, and therefore also a life of continual joy. This is why many Christians regularly practice the sacrament of confession. A Muslim colleague in Egypt once approached my husband and told him, "Do you know the best thing you Christians have? Confession." My husband, surprised, asked him to explain. His colleague told him about being in Lebanon for a training and, troubled by some personal issues, deciding to walk into a random church and confess. "The feeling I had after that was the best I ever had in my life."

Our impressions of what confession should look like often mirror our original images of repentance: tears, sadness, and self-abnegation. And while it can be those things, it can also be joyous. Fr. Tadros Malaty writes:

> Instead of dwelling on your sins, focus on God's love and mercy.
> Thus in your confessions, highlight the positive things that God
> helped you with no matter how small, and avoid crucifying
> yourself because of your sins. Your theme should be: "although I
> am a sinner, God embraced me and I am carried by His hands."[52]

Confession is not just about recounting our sins but recounting our salvation. We have sinned, but our decision to repent and confess is a decision to recognize God's character as a loving Father, ready to embrace us as soon as we return to him.

In addition to regular confession, we can repent daily. Praying the Hours, arrow prayers (more on this in an upcoming chapter), and our personal prayers all offer us the ongoing opportunity to turn away from sin and turn to God. The path to joy is full of thieves ready to steal it from us, but the grace of God offers us protection when we turn to him. Fr. Tadros continues:

> There is no denying that the devil will keep fighting all humans
>
> regardless of their age or status until their last breath. We are in
>
> a constant battle, but our aim is to hide behind our God who will
>
> do the fighting for us.[53]

Indeed, the fact that it is God who is fighting our sins for us gives us a sense of hope, victory, and joy when we repent.

Thus, the second way to practice the joy of repentance is to recognize our repentance as an encounter with Christ, and to allow that encounter to change us from people ashamed to people courageous and victorious. This encounter began at our baptism, when we first entered "from darkness into light, from death into life, from sin into the knowledge of truth, from the worship of idols to the knowledge of the true God," in the words of the Liturgy of Baptism, when we were "buried with Him in baptism, in which you also were raised with Him through faith in the working of God, who raised Him from the dead" (Colossians 2:12). It is the encounter St. Athanasius described when explaining the return of the prodigal son and all the gifts the loving father gave him: "These are the gracious gifts of the Father, by which the Lord honors and nourishes those who abide with Him, and those who return to Him and repent."

The encounter continues with our ongoing participation in the sacramental life of the church—confession, the Eucharist. It continues in the ongoing life of self-giving, of seeing Christ in others, especially in the sick, the poor, the hungry, the naked, and the imprisoned, the way we have discussed in the previous practice. While the shame of sin might keep us solitary, afraid to be seen and known as the Samaritan woman was before she met Christ, practicing the joy of repentance returns us to our community and expands it.

The third way to practice the joy of repentance is to lead others to their own encounters with Christ. For the Samaritan woman, that meant preaching to the whole of Samaria. For each one of us, it will mean different things. For me, this reconciliation begins with my immediate family, taking responsibility for my actions and asking for forgiveness when I have wronged them, sometimes on a daily basis. I then consider the people I interact with, friendships I have neglected, even people I engage with on social media. Perhaps I was not charitable in a conversation about theology—or politics. Perhaps I was disrespectful or dismissive of someone's point of view. I ask God to open my eyes to those instances, and I ask for forgiveness accordingly. My heart is lighter and able to hold more joy when it is empty of anger and hurt toward others.

When I first met my husband's sister, a nun at the Monastery of St. Mercurius in Old Cairo, Egypt, I was surprised at the joyfulness of her demeanor. I had certainly expected that a contemplative nun would be peaceful, calm, and serene, and she was all those things, but she was more than that. She smiled frequently and even occasionally joined in our banter. She greeted us all with warm hugs, and whenever she opened her mouth, it was to share something edifying: something she learned from a sermon she heard, a story she read, or an experience in over a decade of monastic life. Most often she told stories of Mother Erene of Blessed Memory and the advice or the rule she would apply with the sisters. One of her rules was that before every evening prayer, when the nuns gathered together, each sister would say to the other, "I have sinned, forgive me." This daily reconciliation among the nuns of the monastery surely brought about the sense of love and joy I felt on my visits, and it is likely what attracts the thousands of visitors the monastery receives each day. This spirit of reconciliation allows us to encounter Christ.

"With joy you will draw water from the wells of salvation."
   (ISAIAH 12:3, NRSV)

PUT JOY INTO PRACTICE

Denial and defense are our defaults when faced with our own wrongdoing. Symptoms of pride, these are sure to prevent us from experiencing the joy of repentance. The first step toward *metanoia* is putting down our defenses and acknowledging that we have done wrong—and actually do wrong often—for, in the words of Scripture, "all have sinned and fall short of the glory of God" (Romans 3:23). Certain sins we have committed "willingly or unwillingly, knowingly or unknowingly . . . by action, by words, by thought, or by any of our intentions," according to the prayers in the Book of the Hours. The Book of Common Prayer offers repentance "for what we have done and left undone," for not loving God "with our whole heart," and for not loving "our neighbors as ourselves." By these standards, honest self-reflection will reveal that we have sinned daily, often multiple times.

St. Ephraim the Syrian's short prayer of repentance of is a great way to reflect and examine ourselves for repentance. I invite you to pray it with me:

> O Lord and Master of my life, take from me the spirit
> of sloth, despair, lust of power and idle talk. But give
> rather the spirit of chastity, humility, patience and
> love to your servant. Yea, O Lord and King, grant me
> to see my own sins and not to judge my brother, for
> thou art blessed unto the ages and ages. Amen.

If your tradition includes an opportunity for confession, make an appointment as soon as you can. As the date approaches, seek out times to take stock, reflect, and repent on your own as well so that when you go to confession, you're not just talking about your sins, but also about God's work in your life, the embrace of a loving Father.

Take some time to make a list of the people you have wronged and must reconcile with and take the first step toward that reconciliation. Ask for forgiveness when possible and make restitution if necessary. "I have sinned; forgive me" begins a conversation that acknowledges your wrongdoing and makes a request for forgiveness. It is less self-centered than "I'm sorry," which is really about how you feel, not how the other party was wronged. In some cases, such as with immediate family members, this can be done right away. In other cases, this may take time. Seek guidance from a priest, pastor, or other spiritual mentor before opening up old wounds.

Perhaps you already know and have experienced the joy of repentance in your own life. Perhaps, like the woman at the well, you have encountered Christ and have been changed. Take some time, then, to make a list of the people you can invite to an encounter with Christ, and consider how you might do so with humility. Start with your immediate circle and then branch out. Even those who are already in the church sometimes need an invitation.

PRACTICE *Four*

Giving Thanks

"Joyful thanksgiving, so far from being escapist or sentimental, is on the contrary entirely realistic —but with the realism of one who sees the world in God, as the divine creation."
— BISHOP KALLISTOS WARE, *The Orthodox Way*[54]

I never thought a suicide bombing would teach me the true meaning of thanksgiving—until April 19, 2017. On that day, two Coptic Orthodox churches in Northern Egypt suffered explosions that killed at least forty-five worshipers and injured one hundred more. One of the attacks was on a church where His Holiness Pope Tawadros[55] was praying—a clear attempt on the life of the leader of the largest Christian community in the Middle East. The April 2017 attack fell on Palm Sunday, as the Christians of Egypt began their preparations for the upcoming Feast of the Resurrection. The so-called Islamic State of Iraq and Syria (ISIS) claimed responsibility for the attack, one of many that has beset the Copts in Egypt in the past few decades. The irony of the perpetrators' actions is that they did not seem to understand the futility of killing people who believe in the resurrection of the dead.

In fact, that evening during the Eve of Monday Paschal services, while many Christian Egyptians may have stayed home out of fear, many more went to church. The numbers swelled, and the church buildings could not contain them—just as the tomb could not contain Christ. In the words of St. Justin Martyr about the early Christians who suffered persecution, "You can kill, but not hurt us."[56]

Fr. Boules George, the priest of St. Mark's Coptic Orthodox Church on Cleopatra Road in Cairo, one of Egypt's largest churches, addressed the perpetrators of violence with thanksgiving in a widely shared sermon on the evening after the attacks:

> You know why we thank you? I'll tell you. You won't get it, but please believe us. You gave us to die the same death as Christ— and this is the biggest honor we could have. Christ was crucified— and this is our faith. He died and was slaughtered—and this is our faith. You gave us, and you gave them to die. We thank you because you shortened for us the journey.[57]

Surprising as it might sound for a Coptic Orthodox priest to be thanking Islamist terrorists for bombing two churches on Palm Sunday, thanksgiving is a recurring theme in Christianity.

Take a moment and think about the last church service or gathering you have attended. Chances are, it began with the Lord's Prayer, followed by a prayer of thanksgiving. We give thanks before every meal, every hour of the *Agpeya*, and at the start of every liturgy, baptism, wedding, house blessing, unction of the sick, and funeral. I invite you to pray part of the Thanksgiving Prayer together now:

PRACTICE

Four

> Let us give thanks unto the Beneficent and Merciful God, the Father of our Lord, God and Savior, Jesus Christ. For He has shielded us, rescued us, kept us, accepted us unto Him, had compassion on us, supported us, and brought us unto this hour. . . . O Master, Lord, God Almighty, Father of our Lord, God and Savior Jesus Christ, we thank You upon every condition, for any condition, and in whatever condition.

Fr. Daniel Maher prayed these exact words when the bomb detonated in the sanctuary of his church in Tanta, Egypt, killing twenty-five parishioners, including his own son. He attended his son's funeral in the same blood-spattered tunic he wore on Palm Sunday, and he prayed the same prayer of thanksgiving again. And in his pain, he continued to lead his congregation in Pascha week prayers, all the way to the Feast of the Resurrection.[58]

I am learning through his example that when I thank God "in any condition, in every condition, and in whatever condition," I might not be asking God to take me out of a condition of suffering, or even to see a silver lining around that suffering. Rather, I am thanking him in that condition of suffering, and sometimes I might even thank him *for* that suffering. In the words of St. James: "My brethren, count it all joy when you fall into various trials, knowing that the testing of your faith produces patience." (James 1:2–3). God does not purposefully inflict suffering on his children, but it is possible that the suffering I am going through is preventing me from facing worse trials or from committing sin. It could be building in me greater virtues, an increased capacity for prayer, or more empathy toward others who suffer. Thanking God for suffering is not sadism; rather, it is acknowledging that perhaps that suffering can serve a greater purpose.

When my first child had to stay in the neonatal intensive care unit after I was discharged from the hospital, I suffered the pain of leaving the hospital without my baby as many other women with children in the NICU have. I remember sobbing while packing my hospital bag and weeping the entire drive home that night. Yet within that suffering, I found a way to be thankful—my baby was alive; he was receiving treatment and care in the NICU that I would not be able to provide him at home. While I desperately wanted to take him home as soon as possible, I was all the more thankful and joyful when he was discharged from the hospital and I knew I could take him home safely. I thanked God in that suffering, but I would not wish the pain of seeing her child in the NICU on any mother.

During a five-year period of my life, I often traveled to Egypt for work. On every trip, I tried to make the time to visit with my paternal grandmother in the southern part of Egypt, my last living grandparent. During my visits with her, she would retell stories of her younger days, of when she was active, cooking and baking, supervising the fields, and managing the harvest of our family farm. She would then conclude with the words, "But look at me now. I'm old, and tired, and my legs can't carry me like they used to." Yet before she took a breath, she continued, "I thank You, O Lord," kissing both sides of her hands, a traditional way for Egyptians to express thanks to God. I'm not sure when or where that practice originated, but I imagine that kissing the inside of the hand, the palm, where you hold things, is thanksgiving for what you have, and the back of the hand is thanksgiving for what you don't have, or what you don't have control of. It also could mean thanking God for the good (the inside of the hand) and the bad (the outside of the hand) in life.

PRACTICE

Four

My paternal grandmother lived well into her eighties before she passed on. She knew the date of her death, counting the fingers on that same hand she gave thanks with: "One, two, three, four days, and I am traveling. Get me my passport," she said to my uncle. Sure enough, four days later, my cousin found her reposed peacefully in her bed, a few hours after she had eaten breakfast. She had gone on to her eternal rest and her eternal joy—to be with the God to whom she gave thanks in any condition, in every condition, in whatever condition.

Social science continues to prove time and time again that giving thanks leads to joy. Robert Emmons of the University of Miami, who has conducted and compiled multiple studies showing gratitude's positive effects on health,[59] says, "Gratitude rescues us from negativity. . . . Gratitude is our best weapon, an ally to counter these internal and external threats that rob us of sustainable joy."[60] Productivity expert Michael Hyatt cites Emmons in more research that shows gratitude helps us reach our personal and professional goals as well. Hyatt explains this is because "gratitude moves us into a place of abundance—a place where we're more resourceful, creative, generous, optimistic, and kind."[61] Thus, gratitude journals and planners abound on the market to help us remember what we are grateful for (I have one), and one will often find friends doing "thirty days of gratitude" during the month of November on social media, posting comments or sharing photos about the things and people they are grateful for.

For many of us living in the Western Hemisphere, sometimes "giving thanks" is translated as "counting our blessings." Thanking God for all good things acknowledges that "every good and every perfect gift is from above" (James 1:17). It is also an act of humility, acknowledging that what we have is not something we deserve, even if it seems to be the result of our hard work.

Sometimes, however, counting our blessings might give us a sense that we have more favor with God than others and lead us to judge people who have less than we do as having less favor with God. But anyone who has seen the simple joy and happiness expressed on the faces of people who have so much less material wealth than we in developed countries do can attest to the fact that our excess wealth might very well be stealing our joy. Thus, counting our blessings alone is an incomplete form of thanksgiving, though it is important for opening our eyes to God's gracious provision for us, whether material or relational. Taken alone, counting our blessings runs the risk of our being ungrateful when those provisions go away—a job layoff, the loss of a loved one, changing friendships, or social isolation.

In addition, sometimes publicly counting our blessings can cause inadvertent pain to others. We no more deserve our blessings than others deserve their pain. In a recent essay on *Motherwell*, Liz Becker writes:

> When we say we are blessed, when we refer to our marriages or pregnances or children in this way, we say, whether intentionally or not, that we have been arbitrarily chosen for joy, and that all of the suffering in the world has been chosen as well. Every hashtag, every smiling angel emoji, is another tiny arrow aimed at the person who does not have these things, the couple who just failed a third round of IVF, the woman going through her fifth miscarriage, the single man or woman who has struggled through yet another breakup, the parents who have buried a child.[62]

Though Becker argues that perhaps we should credit luck for our blessings, I disagree. The wonder of a newborn child, the

PRACTICE *Four*

excitement of meeting your life partner, the anticipation of a new pregnancy—these are miraculous gifts from God. But those who don't receive those gifts are no less deserving. How do we thank God for our blessings while also showing empathy for those who don't receive the same ones? How can we elevate our practice of thanksgiving to be more than an accounting of what we have?

In her book *Flunking Sainthood*, Jana Reiss points out that gratitude is not only about counting our blessings or appeasing God's desire for it. She discovered that "gratitude didn't save Anne Frank, and it won't save us. It won't heal our diseases, make us rich, or bring us fame. . . . God doesn't owe us anything, no matter how cheerful and uncomplaining we are."[63] Reiss happened upon what gratitude for Christians means in the writings of Thomas Merton, who "suggests that every moment of existence can be a grace. . . . If every moment of existence is a grace, we can simply rest in God. It means our joy might just transcend our circumstances. Happiness in the present moment and joy in God are not the same."[64]

At a recent bridal shower, I struck up a conversation with a woman from my church, whose physician husband, now a sought-after specialist, had recently treated my husband after a car accident. As our conversation went on, she described her first seven years in the United States as "seven years of famine." "There were days," she told me, "that we had to make a decision about whether we should pay our car insurance for that month or buy groceries." As she and her husband adjusted to life in the US, he did his long, low-paying hours of medical residency while she took care of the household and the children. "During that time, I tried to keep a heart of thanksgiving. I knew that if I was not thankful, I would not be able to give joy to my children. I would spend all my energy on negative feelings and have nothing left for them." Seven years of continual thanksgiving despite her circumstances led her to joy in God, a joy that sustains us in times of plenty and in times of poverty.

Fr. Beniameen Morgan, in his book *The Eucharist: A Journey of Repentance*, takes this a step further:

> Eucharist extends in our lives after Communion by sacrifice and
> giving, converting our whole lives into an uninterrupted Eucharist
> for Christ, a sacrifice of thanks and acknowledging His love.[65]

The word *eucharist* itself means "thanksgiving" in Greek, and thus the act of communal thanksgiving extends beyond the *saying* of thanks to the *doing* of thanks—sacrifice and giving.

In the community celebration of thanksgiving through the Eucharist, we are not individually counting our personal blessings, but together thanking God for the greatest gift of all, his body and blood, "given to us for salvation and remission of sins," in the words of the Divine Liturgy. It is a gift for all of us, regardless of our circumstances and thus a gift we can all celebrate. This is quite different from the virtual communal and circumstantial thanksgiving we share on social media that Liz Becker criticizes. Perhaps we should reconsider how we count our blessings publicly. Perhaps, while celebrating the birth of a child, we might quietly offer a prayer for a friend who is suffering from infertility or infant loss. Perhaps, as we celebrate a new engagement or a wedding, we also might pray for our single friends and find a way to ensure their inclusion in our communities. Perhaps, instead of using our phones to Instagram a sumptuous meal, we might use them for an online donation to a local food bank.

There are certainly positive aspects to our public displays of thanksgiving on social media—this is definitely time better spent online than filling the Internet with anger, division, and strife. In addition, thanksgiving is contagious, and a thankful Facebook post sharing good news about a life event can lead to lots of joy as friends celebrate and congratulate from all around the world. The flip side is that others might be scrolling through the "highlight reel" in pain about their own losses and wondering why their own prayers are not being answered.[66]

Perhaps in addition to sharing our thanksgiving for the obvious gifts of children, new jobs, new relationships, and great meals, we might also offer our thanksgiving for situations that are not as obviously positive. How might our conversations change around statements such as, "I just got laid off from my job. Thank God—may he show me what I need to learn through this," or "Along the road that lies beyond my new cancer diagnosis, I am grateful that God is by my side"? Thanksgiving that puts joy into practice is thanksgiving for any condition, in every condition, in whatever condition.

On a trip to Egypt with my husband a few years ago during Holy Pascha Week, we visited a friend who had a bone marrow transplant several years before that his body rejected. His body is now fighting against itself, and over time he will lose more and more of his faculties. The first time I met him he was losing his eyesight; this time he was completely blind and had also lost all of his hair. On our visit, we prayed an hour of the Pascha service of the day, and during the entire visit, he kept giving thanks. His suffering is long, slow, and painful, but he has accepted his lot with thanksgiving. When we had finished praying, he asked my husband to help him find some cassette tapes he was looking for because he was taking a seminary course through distance learning. While others in his situation might be driven away from God, he was drawing closer to him.

Psalm 116:17, prayed during the Ninth Hour of the *Agpeya*, says, "I will offer to You the sacrifice of Thanksgiving, and will call upon the name of the LORD." This verse makes it seem as if being thankful is an act of sacrifice, of giving to God—who has no need for our gifts, who is the giver of all good things. Yet a study of the history of the Eucharistic celebration shows that in the early church, people brought their gifts and laid them at the altar. Some gifts were oblations—wheat and grapes for the bread and wine that would become the body and blood during the celebration of the liturgy, indeed mirroring the sacrifice of thanksgiving outlined in Leviticus 7:12—"Then he shall offer, with the sacrifice of thanksgiving, unleavened cakes mixed with oil, unleavened wafers anointed with oil, or cakes of blended flour mixed with oil." But other gifts were gifts to the Church, for the clergy and the church needs, and alms for the poor.[67]

These days the offerings are not always placed at the feet of the altar every Sunday, but they occur when believers walk into the church and place alms in the offering box before entering the sanctuary. Congregation members still offer oblations by buying flour, Communion wine, and other church necessities, such as cleaning supplies and even toilet paper. They also care for each other's needs, offering their tithes with requests to give them to the poor in the church congregation or in the larger body of Christ. The "giving" of thanksgiving is in this offering. Fr. Athanasius Iskander explains:

> The early Church Fathers saw two inseparable components of the Eucharistic offering: (1) the "gifts" of bread and wine, which represented the first fruit of God's creating, and (2) the *spiritual sacrifices* of mercy (almsgiving), peace (reconciliation), and praise (hymns and prayers of thanksgiving).[68]

In Practice Two we discussed visiting the sick as one of the spiritual sacrifices of mercy, an "almsgiving" of time and effort that leads to joy in the most unexpected ways. The same might be said of all acts of mercy, because they start with the same principle of self-giving. In the previous practice, we discussed how reconciliation can lead others to an encounter with Christ, a response to the joy we experience through repentance and forgiveness. In the last chapter of this book, we will discuss how singing praise also puts joy into practice. These "spiritual sacrifices" offered in the Eucharist turn into gifts of joy to us because of the gift of Christ himself.

What we give to God when we offer thanksgiving, we give to one another. We "give" in the Eucharist out of the abundance of what we have been given by the Great Giver. "Fill our hearts with joy and gladness," St. Basil's Liturgy reads, "that we too having sufficiency always may abound in every good deed." And so, in the practice of our daily lives, after we have celebrated the Divine Liturgy, after we have offered thanksgiving to God for being God, for creating us, and for saving us, we are so overflowing with joy that we can't help giving to others. The outcome of thanksgiving is giving.

The Gospel reading of the Ninth Hour in the *Agpeya* (Luke 9:10–17) illustrates this so clearly. Jesus tells his disciples that they should feed more than five thousand people that had followed him to the mountain to preach. The disciples have no idea where they can get food until one boy (mentioned in John 6:9) makes a small offering—his five loaves and two fish. Christ takes this small sacrifice and, after blessing it, gives his disciples the responsibility of distributing it—making the disciples the givers, even though Christ is the Great Giver. And when all was done, everyone ate their fill, with twelve baskets of leftovers collected.

I've often wondered what they did with all those leftover fragments. I imagine that after they partook of their own meal, they must have asked the crowd, which eventually would return to the "surrounding towns and countryside," to give that food to whoever needed it. Out of the abundance of God's gifts for us, with thanksgiving we give others the good gifts that ultimately come from God himself.

Counting our blessings gives us the sense of happiness we feel when we realize how many things we own, how much we have in a world where many don't. If we stop there, we might be inclined to give others only out of sense of guilt, a "false charity" in the words of Paolo Freire.[69] Offering our thanks to God brings us joy because we realize that what we have to give was given first to us, just as the disciples gave out the food that was multiplied by Christ himself. And so the virtuous cycle continues—in giving, we realize how much we have, so we offer thanks, and in offering thanks, we think about how much we can give.

How then, do we cultivate the attitude of gratitude that leads to joy in God? In addition to weekly participation in the Eucharist, we can give thanks in our daily prayers. When we kneel to pray our personal petitions, we can start a habit of beginning them with thanksgiving, even if just thanks that we are able to turn to God and pray at that moment. Praying the Hours, as we have already discussed, gives us a guide. The Thanksgiving Prayer is prayed before each of the seven Hours, and every Hour ends with an absolution containing a different prayer of thanks—a recipe for constant thanksgiving. Just by praying the morning and evening hours, we have started and ended our days with thanks.

I invite you to pray this prayer of thanksgiving with me, from the absolution of the Eleventh Hour:

Thank you, compassionate Lord, for You granted us to pass this day in peace, brought us thankfully to the night and made us worthy of seeing Your light until sunset.

We can put our gratitude journals to good use, turning our lists of thanks into personal prayers. While there are many beautiful ones on the market, a simple notebook suffices—or even the margins of this book. When I sit down to fill my gratitude journal, I write what I am grateful for as a prayer that begins with "Thank you, God, for . . ." I have found that the structure of the Divine Liturgy gives me a three-part guide to help me go beyond counting my blessings to the thanksgiving that allows me to experience the giving and receiving of sacrificial love—and thus to experience joy.

In the Divine Liturgy, first we thank God for being God. "Giving Him thanks for being God reminds us that God is the creator of all things and in His hands, He holds everything . . . this makes us thank Him for His strong hold over our life, being God," writes Pope Shenouda III.[70] This is the God "before Whom stand the angels, the archangels, the principalities, the authorities, the thrones, the dominions, and the powers," according to the Liturgy of St. Basil. And this is the God who is love itself (see 1 John 4:8). Thus, thanking God for being God also includes thanking him for the love shown to us and the love we share with others, for when we do this we are thanking him for himself.

Take a moment now and write it down:

Thank You, God, for being God.

You can choose your own words to express what that means for you. Here are some of mine:

Thank You, God, for being who you are.

I am thankful because I know you and can speak to you.

The Ninth Hour psalm also gives us words we can use:

Know that the Lord, He is God; It is He who has made us, and not we ourselves; We are His people and the sheep of His pasture. Enter into His gates with thanksgiving, And into His courts with praise. Be thankful to Him, and bless His name. For the LORD is good; His mercy is everlasting; And His truth endures to all generations.

(PSALM 100:3–5)

When we thank God for being God, we can also thank him for the people who make up the fabric of our lives and communities. Where God's family is, he is, and as we thank God for this family, we thank him for being God as well. Soon after the sudden death of a young woman in my church, I watched in awe as my congregation came together in love and support for the grieving family. One woman who showed up to the memorial service had just been discharged from the hospital after a surgery. My husband asked her why she had come in her condition, and she replied, "I cannot leave the family at a time like this." She was not related to the girl's family, but she was part of the church family. The grieving family accepted her condolences with thanksgiving, and this, too, was thanking God for being God and being with us.

We also can give thanks by expressing gratitude toward others directly in any form. One of my favorite ways to do so is in a handwritten thank-you card or letter. St. Paul wrote some of the most eloquent thank-you notes. Consider this one, written at the beginning of his epistle to the church in Thessalonica:

> We give thanks to God always for you all, making mention of you
>
> in our prayers, remembering without ceasing your work of faith,
>
> labor of love, and patience of hope in our Lord Jesus Christ in the
>
> sight of our God and Father. (1 Thessalonians 1:2–3)

I can only wonder at the joy he felt in writing these words and perhaps in imagining the reactions of the Thessalonians when they were read to them. I can only wonder at the power these words of affirmation must have had on the Thessalonians, fledgling Christians in a still largely un-Christian Roman Empire.

We might not be great apostles sending communal thankful epistles to the church congregations we have planted, but we can give thanks for and to others on an everyday basis in our own small ways, and these small ways often add up to great things. When my first two children were baptized, I was too overwhelmed to think about sending thank-you cards to the members of my church community who showered us with kindness and love. However, after my third baby's baptism, I made the effort, writing one or two thank-you cards every night to all who had attended the baptism or had given us gifts on the occasion. It took me a month to write and address the cards, but the result was an overwhelming sense of gratitude and joy every time I completed a few cards.

Writing and sending the cards was more than simply a social obligation. The process reminded me again of the momentous occasion of the baptism, and of the love and generosity of so many people. It was a way of enjoying the occasion and the gifts many times over. As I wrote each card, I thanked God for each person who joined us on such a happy day. The love they shared was God's love, and giving thanks helped me experience it all over again. Thanksgiving is also contagious—an attitude of thanks in one person can spread to many, and so each note of thanks is in itself a gift, affirming the love that others have given.

The second part of the structure of the Divine Liturgy reminds us to thank God for his creation. Every breath of awe and wonder at the beauty of nature or even the ingenuity of humankind is an offer of thanks to God for creating us and the world we enjoy. From the little green clovers peeking through the urban sidewalks of Harlem to the incredible might of Niagara Falls, from the building-block constructions of a toddler to the Great Pyramids of Egypt, these creations and acts of beauty all originate from God. In the Divine Liturgy of St. Gregory, we pray, "You set up the sky for me as a ceiling. You made the earth firm for me so that I could walk on it. For my sake You bridled the sea. For my sake You have revealed the nature of the animals." God created all of this, and he created it for our enjoyment.

"Nature deficit disorder," a term created by Richard Louv, author of *Last Child in the Woods*, describes what he believes to be a major factor in the rise of child obesity, attention disorders, and depression: the decrease in children's direct engagement with nature.[71] I would add that this likely applies to adults as well; I can attest to how quickly direct contact with nature can change our perspectives and moods. Once, on a road trip to Canada, our trip was delayed several hours so we could renew my daughter's passport. By the time we reached our first overnight stop in Maine at 5:00 PM, it was too late to do any of the sightseeing we had planned, and we were all hungry, tired, and out of sorts. Before we headed into our hotel room, I picked up a tourist magazine at the front desk and flipped through it in our room as the kids

PRACTICE *Four*

started changing into their pajamas. I found a historic lighthouse we could visit, and if we left right away, we could still get there on time. My husband quickly agreed, so we gathered our pajama-clad kids into the car and off we went.

Standing safely on solid ground near the lighthouse, as we watched the waves crashing against the docks and breathed in the fresh sea air, all the useless bickering fell away was replaced with the simple enjoyment of God's creation displayed before us. My husband and I embraced as our children ran around and then watched the water in wonder. A huge cruise ship sailed by slowly, to the delight of my older son, who was fascinated by these large ships and how many people they could carry. We met a local, who told us how to reach our destination with less driving by taking a ferry almost as large as one of those cruise ships. Together we watched the sunset, and then drove off to find something to eat. Despite our hunger and exhaustion an hour before, God's wondrous creation restored us. We felt the stab of joy.

Thanking God for his creation is also a powerful profession of faith during a time when many, in word or in deed, reject him as the Almighty *Pantocrator*, creator of heaven and earth, and of all things seen and unseen. While it is easy to assume that this is the purview of a few vocal atheists, many of us who claim to believe in God often easily reject him through our actions: when we misuse God's creation in selfishness and greed, when we engage in the active destruction of natural resources, or even when we squelch the natural curiosity of children. As the Liturgy of St. Gregory continues, "I laid aside Your law by my own opinion."

Let us repent, therefore, of the ways we might have rejected God as the *Pantocrator* in our words or actions. Let us do so by thanking God instead for his creation and his wondrous works. We don't need to travel to see them; many of these works are right outside our windows in the dramatic color-changing leaves of fall, or even right under our noses, in the sweet scent of our babies or the cuddles of our pets. We see them in the electric wires that power our homes and workplaces—or in the palms of our hands, in the phones that put the world at our fingertips and keep us in touch with the ones we love. Have we thought about thanking God for the inventors that made this possible for us? All of these God has made, and we thank him.

If your notebook is still at hand, I invite you to think about the wonders God has made that you have witnessed in your own life today and write them down. Here are some I have written:

Thank you, God, for the fragrant red roses I found growing in my backyard, just when I needed them to give to a friend in the hospital.

Thank you, God, for the chance to see the beautiful waterfalls in Paterson, a glimpse of glory in the middle of a struggling urban community.

Thank you, God, for the people who invented all the medicines that help keep our children healthy.

Psalm 95:2–5 contains another prayer of thanks for God's creation:

Let us come before His presence with thanksgiving;
Let us shout joyfully to Him with psalms.
For the LORD *is* the great God,
And the great King above all gods.
In His hand *are* the deep places of the earth;
The heights of the hills *are* His also.
The sea *is* His, for He made it;
And His hands formed the dry *land*.

The third way the Divine Liturgy points us to thanking God is to thank him for his salvation. If he had not saved us, we would not be able to thank him in every condition, in any condition, in every condition. We would not understand how even suffering can be good if not for Christ's suffering on Good Friday that led to the Resurrection, to hope, to joy. The ultimate example of giving thanks in any condition is Jesus Christ himself at the Last Supper. In the words of retired Archbishop of Canterbury Rowan Williams:

> [I]t is at that moment, when he is looking forward most clearly and vividly to his death, even before the Garden of Gethsemane casts its shadow, that Jesus *gives thanks*. That is, he connects his experience with the reality of God, because that is what thanksgiving does. When we say thank You to God, we connect our own experience with God as Giver.[72]

Liturgical scholar Fr. Daniel Findikyan recounts stories of the Armenians during the Armenian genocide of the early twentieth century who gathered with a priest to celebrate the Eucharist with only a bit of water and some bread crumbs before being herded away to certain death. These are Christians who have met to "give thanks, even in the heart of the darkest experience" in ways I cannot imagine. What I can imagine is the congregation singing, perhaps in soft voices, their concluding hymn after Communion: "We give thanks to you, Lord, who have fed us at your table of immortal life; distributing your body and your blood for the salvation of the world and for life to our souls."[73] Giving thanks in that dark experience gave way to a celebration of life, the life we have in Christ Jesus our Lord, who, in the words of the litany of the Sixth Hour, "filled us all with joy when You came to save the world; Glory be to You."

We can go back into our notebooks and write our thanks to God for his salvation. We can lift up prayers of gratitude for the life we have received through his death and resurrection on a daily basis. We can sing of this salvation in songs of praise as the Psalms do. Yet in thanking God for his salvation, we can also return to the *giving* part of thanksgiving. In thanking him for his ultimate self-sacrifice for us and for our salvation, it only follows that we in turn sacrifice ourselves for others, fulfilling Christ's commandment to "love one another *as I have loved you*" (John 15:12, emphasis added). Regardless of the action, any act of service, any act of mercy, is a prayer of thanksgiving, offered up to God as a sacrifice and returned to the giver as joy.

PUT JOY INTO PRACTICE

Here are some ways to put joy into practice through thanksgiving:

🐾 Chose a daily prayer of thanksgiving. There are several in the Psalms, and I've shared the first part of one I use from the Coptic Orthodox tradition. You might draw from the prayers of another tradition. Choose a prayer and pray it regularly— even when you are not feeling particularly thankful.

🐾 Use a gratitude journal to pen your own personal prayers of thanks. I do this once a week, and I follow the structure of the Divine Liturgy to move from "counting my blessings" to joyful thanksgiving. First, thank God for being God. Second, thank God for his creation; and third, thank him for his salvation.

🦢 Write thank-you cards. Make a list of all the people you'd like to thank. Turn that thanksgiving into a prayer for them and make your thanksgiving contagious.

🦢 Thank God for his salvation by following Christ's ultimate act of self-sacrifice with your own self-sacrifice, turning acts of giving and mercy into a prayer of thanksgiving.

PRACTICE *Four*

PRACTICE *Five*

Hospitality

Receiving guests was an act of love toward a brother that was more valued than any ascetical practice and was in line with biblical and monastic principles of loving your neighbor as yourself.
—Tamav Lois Farag[74]

ook at all the sparklies, Momma!" my toddler exclaimed with glee as the Christmas lights in our neighborhood began to go up in late November. I love the twinkling lights of the season, especially as the days get shorter, the nights get longer, and the weather gets colder here in the Northeast. It's fitting that as the world outside becomes more and more inhospitable, we welcome the Advent of our Lord with the lights and decorations in our homes.

We all know that the opposite happened on the day of the Nativity. The homes and even the inns had no room for a traveling man and his young, pregnant wife. The Mother of God gave birth to the Incarnate Logos in a manger, where the animals served as birth attendants, and shepherds with their sheep came to worship. Yet there, fittingly, the angels could proclaim joy to the world (Luke 2:10).

It might be said that Mary herself offered the first act of hospitality to the Lord. In the words of St. Athanasius of Alexandria, "He, the Mighty One, the Artificer of all, Himself prepared this body in the virgin as a temple for Himself, and took it for His very own, as the instrument through which He was known and in which He dwelt."[75] Her acceptance of God's will allowed him to dwell in her, and through her enter the world and dwell in all of us. St. Athanasius, in fact, explains the Incarnation in terms of hospitality:

> You know how it is when some great king enters a large city
> and dwells in one of its houses; because of his dwelling in that
> single house, the whole city is honored, and enemies and robbers
> cease to molest it. Even so is it with the King of all; He has come
> into our country and dwelt in one body amidst the many, and in
> consequence the designs of the enemy against mankind have been
> foiled and the corruption of death, which formerly held them in
> its power, has simply ceased to be.[76]

This one act of hospitality literally saved the world. By his becoming incarnate of St. Mary, all of humankind is honored, and by his coming he abolished death, the great enemy of joy.

The Theotokos's acceptance of the will of God at the Annunciation birthed more acts of hospitality, and with every act, joy. Upon learning of her cousin Elizabeth's pregnancy, Mary, pregnant herself, travels to her home to serve her. When she arrives, Elizabeth tells her, "As soon as I heard the sound of your greeting, the child in my womb leaped for joy" (Luke 1:44, NRSV). Everywhere Christ is present there is joy, even when he was in the womb of his mother. And thus, in the very definition of hospitality in Christianity, opening the doors of our homes to others means opening our doors to God himself.

There are other, more expanded understandings of hospitality, but for this practice, I focus on the hospitality that involves inviting others into our homes. I don't think it's a coincidence that Christ's metaphor for the kingdom of heaven takes the form of his "Father's house" having "many mansions" (John 14:2), and the practice of hospitality in people's homes is central to the Christian tradition, and so this chapter focuses on homes— spaces of intimacy—where connection and belonging can happen in very personal ways.

Hospitality was the hallmark of the earliest Christians, even among the hermits who left the world to live ascetic lives in the desert. *The Sayings of the Desert Fathers* (translated by Benedicta Ward, SLG)[77] contains approximately forty instances of the word *joy* (or *joyfully*), half of them in the context of receiving a visitor. "When they arrived" to Abba Moses's cell, "the Abba welcomed them joyfully and then took leave of them with delight." When Abba Macarius visited Abba Antony, he was left waiting patiently at the door until "later, seeing his patience, he opened the door and received Macarius with joy, saying to him, 'I have wanted to see you for a long time, having heard about you.'" Visitors were received by the desert fathers as if they were receiving Christ himself.

The Christian monastic tradition began in the Egyptian desert, and its tradition of hospitality still lives today, not just in Egypt but almost everywhere monasticism is practiced. The hospitality of the desert fathers and mothers stands in stark contrast to what we imagine hospitality to look like now. Today our dinner tables must be social media worthy, with elegant place settings, time-consuming decorations, and lavish feasts.

Hospitality in the Egyptian desert looked markedly different. Monks offered visitors what they had, usually dried bread and some lentils, and perhaps a bit of fruit if it were available. Their cells were often bare, save for the work they did with their hands and some books. Yet these cells were often prepared for visitors. On a tour of the Monastery of St. Macarius in Egypt, I noticed that the ancient cells there had two small chambers: an inner room where a monk might sleep and say his prayers, and an outer room where he could receive guests.

It's another paradox. These people left the world to live solitary lives with God in the desert, yet the very architecture of their cells set them up to welcome guests. Rather than seeing guests as interruptions to their ascetic monastic rule, they welcomed them with joy as though receiving Christ himself. St. John Cassian, a monk who studied Egyptian ascetism in the fourth century, writes about his visits to the "elders," the Egyptian monastics:

> Except in the case of the regular days, Wednesdays and Fridays, wherever we went the daily fast was broken. When we asked why the daily fast was thus ignored by them without scruple one of the elders replied, "The opportunity for fasting is always with me. But as I am going to conduct you on your way, I cannot always keep you with me. . . . And so receiving Christ in you I ought to refresh Him, but when I have sent you on your way I shall be able to balance the hospitality offered for His sake by a stricter fast on my own account. For "the children of the bridegroom cannot fast while the bridegroom is with them" but when he has departed, then they will rightly fast.[78]

The elder refers here to Matthew 9:14–17, when John's disciples question Jesus about why the Pharisees fast so much, but his disciples don't. Jesus answered, "Can the friends of the bridegroom mourn as long as the bridegroom is with them? But the days will come when the bridegroom will be taken away from them, and then they will fast." Sr. Benedicta Ward similarly quotes another desert father in her introduction to *The Sayings:* "A brother said, 'Forgive me, father, for I have made you break your rule,' but the old man said, 'My rule is to receive you with hospitality and send you on your way in peace.'"[79]

The birth of coenobitic, or community monasticism, in contrast to the hermit monasticism the desert fathers were known for, begins with a story of radical hospitality. After enlisting in the emperor's army in the fourth century, Pachomius and his soldiers descended upon the Egyptian city of Thebes (what is now modern-day Luxor) and were welcomed by the villagers with food and shelter. The pagan Pachomius, astounded by the love shared by these Christian villagers, converted to Christianity. Three years later he became a monk, and when a community of monks developed around him, he began to set down rules for common life and mutual service, eventually developing the *Pachomian Koinonia,* an order of monasticism based on communal living rather than the hermit style. The Benedictine order in the West, widely known for its longstanding practice of hospitality, is based on this.[80]

The Pachomian story demonstrates the ability for Christian hospitality to transform the receiver, but it also transforms the giver—in fact, it transforms everyone and everything. In the words of Tamav Lois Farag, "The hospitality of each person can transform any society."[81] St. John Chrysostom describes what happens to our homes when we open them to visitors:

Let us receive the Saints, that the house may shine, that it may be freed from choking weeds, that the bed-chamber may become a haven. . . . Receive them then with readiness of mind, bringing as they do ten thousand blessings to you, through the greeting of peace.[82]

From the desert fathers we learn how hospitality brings joy in its simplicity. We welcome the visitor with joy and offer what we have. St. John Chrysostom notes that "he does not require you to kill a calf, but only to give bread to the hungry, raiment to the naked, shelter to the stranger."[83] To me, this translates today to avoiding exhausting myself with the preparation of a fancy and expensive feast. A simple meal, warmly offered, is enough.

I learned that lesson from another story of hospitality—the story of Mary and Martha. Unlike the inns of Bethlehem thirty years prior, these sisters and their brother Lazarus regularly welcomed the Savior into their home. The story is well known, but it is worth revisiting from the perspective of hospitality.

Now it happened as they went that He entered a certain village; and a certain woman named Martha welcomed Him into her house. And she had a sister called Mary, who also sat at Jesus' feet and heard His word. But Martha was distracted with much serving, and she approached Him and said, "Lord, do You not care that my sister has left me to serve alone? Therefore tell her to help me." And Jesus answered and said to her, "Martha, Martha, you are worried and troubled about many things. But one thing is needed, and Mary has chosen that good part, which will not be taken away from her." (Luke 10:38–42)

PRACTICE *Five*

I've often wondered why Martha wasn't honored for her labor of love. After all, the Son of God was in her home, and she was serving him. He was likely also with his disciples, so this was a party of at least thirteen guests, and worse yet, she wasn't getting any help. As an older sibling and now as a mother, I can identify with the resentment she was feeling. St. Cyril of Alexandria's commentary on this passage is what illuminated me:

> But let those who open to them their house, meet them cheerfully, and with alacrity, and as their fellows; and not so much as those who give, but as those who receive: as those who gain, and not as those who expend. And the more so as they profit doubly; for in the first place they enjoy the instruction of those they hospitably entertain; and secondly, they also win the reward of hospitality.[84]

Martha saw herself as the giver, the one who expends. Mary understood that Jesus's coming meant that she should receive, that she should gain. Martha chose what was good—to serve—but Mary chose what was better—to connect, and to connect with no less than the Son of God visiting her home.

I have been guilty many times of corralling myself in the kitchen when guests arrive, making one more cup of coffee or preparing one more dessert, only to hear my guests protest, "Get out of the kitchen and sit down! We came here to spend time with you!" My coffee is good, but connection is better. Connection is where we learn from each other, where we experience the joy of God's presence. True, meaningful, authentic connection is something we are starving for, even as we are more and more virtually connected in our online worlds. Worldly hospitality might have us discussing the weather or the source of our stemware and never building a connection that goes deeper. The kind of hospitality that brings joy is the one that goes deeper, opening the door for vulnerability and authenticity. In the words of *The Paraclete Book of Hospitality*:

> Hospitality is the crux of being open with each other: what greater joy is there than entering into another person's life, sharing the pain and the joy, being accepted and accepting the other as a brother or sister in the Lord.[85]

My friend Amy and her husband, Nader, attend a large Coptic Orthodox church that has regularly welcomed immigrants and asylum seekers from Egypt into the congregation in increasing numbers over the past two decades. To help the newcomers feel more welcome, once a month Amy would hold a "koshary night," when she would make a massive amount of a common but absolutely delectable Egyptian meal called "koshary," made up of rice, black lentils, macaroni, fried onions, chick peas, and garlicky tomato sauce. She would invite any newcomers that had arrived that month, and after everyone had assembled their dish, she would ask each one to share the story of their journey to the United States. With great joy, Amy shared with me how some of those stories would bring tears—stories of family left behind and challenges to overcome—but also hope at the beginning of something new. Often these gatherings resulted in forged connections and shared solidarity. It also turned these new arrivals into guests. The church had many services for them—health care, English classes, legal help—but these gatherings allowed these newcomers to feel like more than mere clients or recipients of services but like members of the church family, affirmed in their humanity.

Scholar of early Christian hospitality Amy Oden points out that hospitality was also very important in the early church because of how dangerous it was to travel alone in those days. Travelers faced all manner of risks from thieves and bandits, with great exposure to the elements by road and sea. The Parable of the Good Samaritan illustrates these risks clearly. While in the twenty-first century it may be physically safer to travel alone now, at least in developed countries, in many ways travelers are still vulnerable to a different kind of danger: the danger of loneliness. Whether travel is for a short period or for a complete relocation to a new environment, loneliness is a great risk. In many ways, we are traveling alone even as we are surrounded by people.

Loneliness is the disease of our generation, affecting mental and physical health in ways that are now receiving special focus in the medical field. The American Psychiatric Association lists several studies linking loneliness to physical and mental health. It affects and is affected by depressive symptoms and is associated with risk of Alzheimer's disease. It increases stress hormones and blood pressure, disrupts sleep, and even increases the risk of heart attacks.[86]

The effects of community and connection change all this. Recently, the preliminary outcomes of a health trial conducted in the English town of Frome showed dramatically improved health outcomes when isolated people become connected to communities. Hospitality brings about healing because it helps to create this community.[87] "God sets the lonely in families," the psalmist says (Psalm 68:6, NIV), after exhorting the reader to "rejoice before him— his name is the LORD" (v. 4). In the words of Juliana Schmemann, "To pay attention to lonely people is a mission."[88] Hospitality can bring about authentic connection, and through that connection we can save each other from the danger of traveling alone.

The first way to build authentic connection through hospitality is to listen, to find ways to share our stories, to truly hear one another and empathize with each other. My friend Amy did just that through her "koshary nights," and as we look around in our own communities and consider to whom we might open our doors, we will find our own ways to listen to each other. You might ask your visitor to share an experience or something he or she learned recently.

Opening our doors to others requires effort from us. Not every gathering will be emotional and life-changing. Not every visitor will be entertaining or even necessarily pleasant. Some conversations will be boring, even irritating. But everyone needs a listening ear, everyone has a story, and everyone needs rest on the journey.

The second way to build authentic connection through hospitality is to allow others the blessing and dignity of giving. In the past, when I've invited people over to my house and they asked what they could bring, I used to respond, "Nothing, just come," because I really just wanted their company. I used to believe I was being magnanimous, but I now realize that in a way I was being selfish. When opening the doors of hospitality, it is wise to allow the guest to also feel like a giver. It turns the gathering into sharing. Now, when guests ask, "What can I bring," I request something, however small—fruit, juice, soda, paper cups, a loaf of bread—or I tell them to bring whatever they would like to bring. Sometimes, without prompting, whatever they bring is exactly what is needed in ways I could not have predicted. Once I invited a friend over for dinner. Although she herself had no children, she had the foresight to bring a few toys from the dollar store for my children. This occupied them for several hours, enough time to allow us to share in some adult conversation that both she and I needed. Allowing the guest to be the giver paves the way for connection and for seeing Christ in the person who visits, rather than seeing the visitor as a receiver of charity and the visitor feeling beholden.

Amy Oden describes how hospitality changes us—that, in fact, the mark of true hospitality, or in her words, "gospel hospitality," is repentance:

> When we welcome others, something happens to us. We are changed by the welcome we offer, as God fills and reorients our hearts. This decentering and reframing is the very movement the New Testament calls *metanoia*, or turning, usually translated "repentance." This turning and repentance occurs not only in the interior landscape of the individual, but also in the exterior landscape of the community. As communities become more hospitable they experience a turning, too. While it may not always be easy, the mark of repentance assures us we are on the path of gospel hospitality.[89]

Offering hospitality is another opportunity for an encounter with Christ, the kind of encounter the Samaritan woman had when she met him at the well. Christ seems initially to be the visitor, a Jew in Samaria, a stranger at the well, asking the Samaritan woman for a drink of water, "only to become the host himself, offering her living water," as Amy Oden puts it. Similarly, Zacchaeus the tax collector experiences his own *metanoia* when Christ dines in his home. He turns from his ways of extortion to restoration, vowing to give half his money to the poor and return any taxes he collected by false accusation fourfold (see Luke 9). When we welcome a visitor into our homes, we welcome Christ, and when Christ visits, we encounter him and he changes us.

My longtime friend Maria experienced this kind of encounter when she recently spent a year in Greece working with refugees fleeing the civil war and unrest in Syria, Afghanistan, and other parts of the world. She shared with me how she felt the most joy *outside of* work, visiting families without her aid worker hat on. During those visits, they shared experiences of happier days in Syria, discussed spiritual topics, or simply played cards over tea. In Maria's experience, everyone was both the guest and the host. Maria served the refugees through her work as the refugees received the host country's hospitality, and yet, when she visited their homes, those same refugees gave *her* refuge. Neither Maria nor those families needed to travel alone.

Outside of a refugee camp, where does one begin when deciding to open one's home to others so that Christ may come in? Who are those "others"? Surely hospitality goes beyond inviting our family and friends over. For me, one of the first steps is to seek out those who might literally be "traveling alone." When I was growing up, my parents often met new immigrants from Egypt at the airport. Before taking them to their apartments or hostels where they would start their new lives, my parents would bring them to our home first for a meal and listen to the stories of their journeys. Occasionally someone would arrive with no place to go initially, especially single women who found it more difficult to find lodging, and so they would stay with us for a time. This became a model for me. In those days, new immigrants came on immigration visas. Now, many come as refugees, seeking political or religious asylum, their journeys even harder and their struggles upon arrival more difficult.

Jesus Christ himself entered Egypt as a refugee, after St. Joseph was told in a dream to flee to Egypt because Herod sought to "destroy Him" (Matthew 2:13). In the Coptic Orthodox Church, the Feast of Our Lord's Entry into Egypt is celebrated as one of the seven minor feasts, an event obviously significant to the ancient church of Egypt. Yet the feast is celebrated not as a commemoration of Egypt's hospitality to the Holy Family, but as Christ's blessing to the land of Egypt, and a fulfillment of the prophecy, "On that day there will be an altar to the LORD in the center of the land of Egypt, and a pillar to the LORD at its border" (Isaiah 19:19, NRSV). Indeed, Deir El-Maharraq, where it is said that the Holy Family settled for six months, is located at the center of Egypt on the map, and the altar stone in the ancient church there is said to stand right where Christ himself was laid. Church tradition tells us that his time in Egypt led to the crumbling of Egypt's idols, and sixty years later Egypt would accept the Gospel of Christ through the preaching of St. Mark the Evangelist. The *metanoia* of an entire nation began with the welcome of a refugee family.

Some churches have welcomed refugee families by preparing their new apartments for them, furnishing them and providing toys and other needs. Perhaps we can also invite that refugee family into our own homes for a meal and help them find healing after their arduous journey.

Refugees and immigrants are not the only ones that might be traveling alone. Do you live in a college town? Invite a student who is far from his or her family over for a meal. Look out for those students who cannot go home for the holidays and give them the opportunity to celebrate the holidays with you. Perhaps there are many professionals who move to your area for work, away from their hometowns and their families. I remember being one of those myself, when I took a job in Washington, D.C., after college in New York. As I tried to navigate the new world of adulthood and independence, the excitement of a new job and a new city, I cried every night for the first two weeks. The nightly tears subsided through the hospitality of others, some young professionals like myself, and others older, wiser, and happy to share their homes and their experiences with me. They were able to look beyond my façade of self-sufficiency and realize that I needed, as everyone does, a sense of belonging. Look around your community for the individual wayfarers or the new families, connect with them, help them build a sense of belonging, and help them heal from the wounds and dangers they've experienced on their journeys.

The Gospel reading of the Eleventh Hour of the *Agpeya* tells us a story of hospitality and healing. It is prayed at sunset, right around the time when someone might be invited over for dinner:

> After leaving the synagogue he entered Simon's house. Now Simon's mother-in-law was suffering from a high fever, and they asked him about her. Then he stood over her and rebuked the fever, and it left her. Immediately she got up and began to serve them. As the sun was setting, all those who had any who were sick with various kinds of diseases brought them to him; and he laid his hands on each of them and cured them. Demons also came out of many, shouting, "You are the Son of God!" But he rebuked them and would not allow them to speak, because they knew that he was the Messiah. (Luke 4:38–41, NRSV)

I'm struck by the mother-in-law's immediate response to her healing. She did not demand that her daughter or son-in-law continue to wait on her as she recovered. Rather, she "immediately" got up and served them. Christ's healing was immediate and complete, and I can't help imagining that her swift response was the result of thanksgiving and joy. "Jesus himself is in my house!"

she might have exclaimed when she realized that her fever had left her and it was Jesus who healed her. "Let's celebrate his presence!" After Christ healed her, the doors of that home remained open for the healing of others—"all those who had any who were sick . . . brought them to him." Everyone in need of healing found healing in this home because Christ was there.

Here Jesus Christ gives us a model, not only of how to be hospitable toward guests, but how to receive another's hospitality. Many of us who have opened our homes to others have not become accustomed to accepting the hospitality of others. And yet we see how Christ, the great Giver who has prepared a home for us in his Father's house where "there are many dwelling places" (John 14:2, NRSV), humbled himself to accept the service of others. More than that, he became a healing presence in every home he visited, a bearer of joy, not burden. This is our model for accepting hospitality from others.

Bring joy by accepting the love offered graciously. Offer help where help can be offered. Play with the children and listen to their repetitive or even ridiculous stories as if you are hearing them for the first time. Share your own story, a new song, a passage you have read from the Bible or another book that has recently inspired you. Bring a friend in need of hospitality as well.

When my father was a graduate student at Union Theological Seminary, we were invited to eat dinner in the apartment of another seminarian named Tom and his wife, Roseann. I was probably seven or eight years old, and it was one of my first intimate experiences with Christians outside of my own tradition. They said grace differently than we did, but I felt welcome. Over dinner, Roseann learned that my mother was usually alone with us children all day (there were three of us at the time), isolated and still adjusting to a new country while my father was in his classes or studying.

So, Roseann started visiting us on a regular basis, checking in on my mom and offering her companionship and English language practice as my mom offered her tea. I remember looking forward to Roseann's visits, and although we have lost touch with her and Tom since they graduated back in the 1980s, I long to be able to thank her for being a hostess and a visitor at the same time, for extending a welcome and sharing love with our family. I remember Roseann with joy.

I'll never forget the first Thanksgiving we ever hosted at my house, when I became an adult able to host others. Thanksgiving often falls on or near the Commemoration of St. Mina the Wonderworker,[90] one of the patron saints of my congregation. That year on the Coptic calendar, his commemoration fell on Thanksgiving Day, so we decided to have our feast in the early afternoon immediately after the Divine Liturgy at church so people could join us and still participate in any evening invitations if they had any. We invited anyone we saw at church that day, but especially people we knew would be working at night, people who had recently immigrated to the US, or people who were only in town for a short visit.

The turkey was undercooked. The roast beef I made was a little tough. But everyone left with smiles on their faces. They enjoyed each other's company, and the mulled apple cider came out perfectly. The house was full and warm with everyone's fellowship; we shared prayers and stories. After enjoying the Eucharist together at church, we gathered in thanksgiving and hospitality, and there was a palpable sense of joy in the room. I did not want people to leave, but even when they did, I still felt joy. It had settled into our home and over us.

You carry all the ingredients
To turn your existence into joy.
Mix them.
—HAFIZ

PRACTICE

Five

PUT JOY INTO PRACTICE

Hospitality is truly the giving and experiencing of self-sacrificial love, a real way to experience and give joy. I invite you to take a moment now to put joy into practice and identify who in your community might be traveling alone. Here are some people to consider:

- College students
- Young professionals
- A newly married couple
- A new family that has moved into town or joined your congregation
- Elderly people who still live in their homes
- Neighbors
- Military families

Keep in mind that invitations might be turned down on the first try—sometimes people don't want to impose, sometimes this is related to culture, and sometimes people don't want to be considered charity cases. Without being too pushy, don't be deterred by the veneer of independence—everyone needs community; everyone needs to experience joy.

I once had an elderly next-door neighbor who lived alone and was fiercely independent. Once on a summer evening, my children wanted to play outside in the front yard, where they prefer to play so other kids on the block can come out and join them. I sat on the front porch with a book to read as I watched them play, and I decided to order a pizza for dinner. My elderly next-door neighbor came over in her walker and sat down to chat. The pizza arrived and she joined us in a spontaneous dinner together. I brought out a watermelon for us to share while we enjoyed conversing and watching the kids play. I thought nothing more of it until a week later the same neighbor came by to tell me that the day she had pizza with us would have been her sixtieth wedding anniversary with her late husband, and she had been feeling depressed. Our simple and effortless act of hospitality lifted her spirits.

Sometimes discovering who needs hospitality is a matter of taking a few moments to sit outside, linger on your front porch, or say hello to the neighbor living on the same floor in your apartment building. We might feel overwhelmed by great needs of the world presented to us on the news, but it is our simple acts of hospitality that will change the world, not our worries. Absorbed in our own lives, schedules, and concerns, it can be easy to overlook those nearby who need our open doors. They might not be refugees escaping civil war, but they certainly might be fighting their own invisible battles. Our homes can be a place of peace and refuge.

If deciding when, how, and with whom to begin opening the doors to hospitality is daunting or overwhelming, begin with the people you know and are already comfortable with. Invite them for coffee, tea, or supper, and then enlist their help in being hospitable together. Together, identify who in your circles is in need of community, who is traveling alone, and set up a small gathering. As Christ himself says, "For where two or three are gathered together in My name, I am there in the midst of them" (Matthew 18:20). There can be no greater joy.

PRACTICE *Six*

Arrow
Prayers

The beginners in prayer . . . will find many obstacles to frustrate and quench the life of prayer, such as despair, sleepiness, weakness, headaches and the heavy weight of sin . . . but . . . in order for a rocket to be launched in space it requires a huge amount of fuel to give it the necessary propulsion and thrust to overcome the gravitational force; but when it reaches its orbit in space it needs very little fuel to maintain its speed. Hence, if we get rid of the heaviness and weakness resulting from our sins, prayer will carry us up easily heavenward, praising and glorifying God.

—FR. MARCUS BISHAY OF BLESSED MEMORY[91]

T his is the worst we've ever seen," the man said that morning, as he and his coworkers, wearing gloves and hazmat uniforms, started transporting our belongings outside beside the dumpster parked in our driveway. For insurance purposes, I would have to inventory every single, foul-smelling item before they threw it in the dumpster and hauled it away.

Our basement had flooded, but not with river or rainwater. It had flooded with the entire town's raw sewage. Almost every item on the floor of our ground-level basement, which we had been using as our home office, playroom, and laundry room, had been contaminated by sewage—clothes, toys, books, files, furniture— and the stench was so rotten and so hazardous to our health, we could not live there until it was cleaned up. We called our home-owners insurance company and booked a hotel room, taking up residence there for a week until our basement could be completely gutted, cleaned, and sanitized.

After our second night at the hotel, my husband and I went back to the house. We surveyed the piles of soiled belongings we would have to sort through wearing masks and gloves in the snowy March weather. My husband started rearranging our upstairs furniture to accommodate our new living situation, minus the basement. I got on the phone with our insurance company and learned that our policy might not cover all the damage and all the losses—perhaps not even one quarter of it. As my heart sank with every word the insurance agent said, I could still smell the stench from the basement, and a sense of being completely overwhelmed swept over me.

I left the house and walked to where my car was parked at a neighbor's house to get a breath of fresh air. As worry and anxiety flooded me, these words flowed out of my lips:

Save me, O God, for the waters have come up to my neck.

This prayer shot up like an arrow to God, and I felt relief right away. My anxious thoughts subsided, and I could feel the tension in my shoulders releasing. My problem was big, overwhelming, and exhausting. I didn't get an immediate miracle, but I was reminded that God was with me, and that I could call upon him as I worked through this minor crisis. I settled into repeating a few times a more commonly known arrow prayer, the Jesus Prayer:

> My Lord Jesus Christ, Son of the Living God,
> have mercy upon me, a sinner.

I returned to my house, now feeling overwhelmed not by anxiety, but by joy. The house still contained the stench of sewage, the living room packed with large black bags of belongings salvaged from the contaminated basement. None of this brought me joy, but those few minutes with God did. The situation still took months to sort out between the insurance company, the mitigation company, the municipality, and a few legal consultations, and even now, over a year later, our house has still not been fully restored. The arrow prayers did not magically solve all the problems, but they solved the essential one: the sense that these problems and tasks were too much for me, that I could not handle them, that I was alone, afraid, and drowning.

Since my childhood, my father of confession had advised me to pray "arrow prayers" in times of need. These prayers helped me settle anxious thoughts before bed, battle sinful thoughts, or deal with difficult people. I learned about arrow prayers again in Sunday School, and specifically about the most well-known arrow prayer in the Orthodox Church, the Jesus Prayer. Practicing arrow prayers is a way to pray without ceasing, part of the Pauline recipe for joy: "Rejoice always, pray without ceasing, in everything give thanks; for this is the will of God in Christ Jesus for you" (1 Thessalonians 5:16–18, NRSV).

While arrow prayers can be traced back to Old Testament times, their regular practice in Christianity was introduced to us by the desert fathers. Besides the Jesus Prayer, Lois Farag describes a few other examples:

> It is said about Abba Serapion that he would advise new monks to pray the one simple prayer, "Lord, teach me to do Thy will." St. Macarius of Egypt has also said, "There is no need at all to make long discourses; it is enough to stretch out one's hands and say, 'Lord, as you will, and as you know, have mercy.' And if the conflict grows fiercer say, 'Lord, help!'" [92]

Abba Isaiah advised his novices who were struggling with temptation to repeat, "Be willing to help me, O Lord, because I am weak and cannot keep up this battle." Abba Sisoes often repeated, "Lord Jesus, protect me against my tongue." [93]

St. John Cassian's favorite arrow prayer came from Psalm 70:1—"*Make haste, O God, to deliver me! Make haste to help me, O* LORD!" He advises using it in all circumstances:

> For someone who needs help in all things is making clear that he requires the help of God not simply in hard and sad situations but equally and amid fortunate and joyful conditions. He knows that God saves us from adversity and makes our joys linger and that in neither situation can human frailty survive without His help. [94]

In his historical review of arrow prayers, Irénée Hausherr derives a definition based on St. John Cassian's explanation: "a formula that can easily be repeated several times a day by people who are preoccupied with other tasks." [95] All arrow prayers were considered an invocation of the sacred name of Jesus, whether or not the formula actually contained his name. Calling on his name is a matter of inner disposition, focusing on the direction of prayer rather than the specific wording.

Arrow prayers serve two functions: reaching out to God in times of need, as Abba Macarius describes, and ongoing, unceasing prayer, as St. Paul prescribes (see 1 Thessalonians 5:17). Origen of Alexandria explains how to fulfill the command for unceasing prayer:

> The man who prays continually is the man who combines prayer with necessary works and works with prayer. This is the only way it seems possible to fulfill the precept of unceasing prayer. We have to envision the whole life of a pious Christian as one long prayer, and the exercise we commonly refer to as prayer is merely a part of the whole.[96]

And thus, despite being introduced to the world as a common practice by the desert monastics, arrow prayers are for all of us, helping us to turn every aspect of our lives into an opportunity to connect with God through prayer—while waiting for the train on a morning commute, while gardening, while standing in an elevator, while cooking a meal for visitors, while waiting in line at the grocery store, while cleaning the toilet—all of these are opportunities to experience God's presence in us through prayer, and arrow prayers give us a tool to do so. I have used situations like those for spontaneous, personal prayers, but I have found that I remember to pray these personal prayers much more often when I already have been repeating an arrow prayer. These days, when we find ourselves waiting, we fill the time by looking at our smartphones, checking our social media feeds or our emails, making every moment a constant input of information—often information we cannot control or tasks we cannot take action on while in line or sitting in traffic. This can add to our general sense of stress and lack of control.

I am guilty of this. Once, standing in line at the pharmacy, I opened Facebook on my phone and found out about the death of a friend's father after a long battle with Alzheimer's disease and cancer. I knew I needed to reach out to that friend, but it was my turn to request my medications at the register, so I did not even get the chance to lift up a silent prayer for her. I spent the drive home anxious to get on the computer to write her a note, knowing that she was in the midst of funeral arrangements and would not be able to take a call. My time in line at the pharmacy would have been better spent praying a few arrow prayers. I would find out about the death soon enough, at a better time and location to reach out to my friend. Using arrow prayers can help us reclaim control of our time and energy. Information overload drains us, but prayer fills us.

Arrow prayers also prepare us for other fruitful times of prayer. Lois Farag explains how this works practically:

Since we are constantly in [God's] presence, we should constantly bless and praise him. We do not praise God only when the liturgy or other communal prayer starts. We do not attend a meeting and start by saying, "Well, let me see where to start, I am not sure what I should be speaking about." Rather we prepare for the meeting in advance and then just before the meeting starts we gather our thoughts to be ready for discussion. The same should be true for prayer. . . . That is why the fathers considered praying without ceasing to be the entry point to start our prayers. Praying without ceasing is preparing for prayer.[97]

Arrow prayers help us to pray without ceasing through their repetition and their ease, and through them we become ready to meet God and feel the joy of his presence. The desert fathers had these prayers on their lips at all times—while working with their hands, while tidying their cells, even while sitting with visitors. Monastics and non-monastics alike keep prayer ropes or prayer beads around their wrists or in their pockets to finger and count out their arrow prayers, especially if they have designated special times to do so. Fr. Matta Al-Maskeen (Fr. Matthew the Poor) writes in *Guidelines to Prayer* that praying in this way slowly changes us. "For the frequent looking up to Christ in prayer impresses our inner being the invisible image of Christ—that is, His attributes, His exquisite sweetness and the light of His face."[98]

Arrow prayers can provide us with inner stillness during times of turbulence. Those few minutes I spent in arrow prayers while dealing with the sewage gave me so much joy because not only had I spent a few minutes in the presence of God, but through those prayers he had imprinted himself in my heart in some small way. We often joke about how difficult experiences "give us gray hairs" or cause wrinkles on our faces, but when these adverse circumstances are met with prayer and trust in God, we can avoid having those experiences imprint our hearts. Through arrow prayers, what is imprinted instead is God himself.

Because using arrow prayers to experience the joy of God's presence in my life has been so effective for me, I became curious about how my contemporaries use arrow prayers and whether those prayers have helped them in their lives. Naturally, I turned to social media and asked that very question on my blog, my Facebook page, and in a few groups.

I've heard many stay-at-home moms talk about the Jesus Prayer being a lifeline, helping them get through the day with the challenges of raising multiple children. Rania changes the end of the Jesus Prayer to suit the current need: "My Lord, Jesus Christ, son of the Living God, give me patience (so I don't go crazy on my kids)!"

Kelsey spoke of a prayer her spiritual father gave her to pray when she was battling anxiety:

> I have a small prayer I use in my day-to-day devotion that has aided me greatly. I suffer from anxiety and depression, and my spiritual father was instrumental in giving me my greatest weapon against them: "Let all adverse powers be banished beneath the sign of the image of the cross." While saying this prayer I cross my forehead using the tip of my thumb, followed by my lips, and finish off with a full sign of the cross. It's a verbal and physical reminder of God's presence and his life-giving cross.

While those suffering from clinical anxiety and depression are right to seek therapeutic and medical treatment, it is important not to neglect the spiritual side of therapy, and that's where an elder or a spiritual father can help complete the picture. Our Western culture is now only beginning to acknowledge the role spirituality plays in physical and psychological healing.

Frederica Mathewes-Green points this out in her book *The Jesus Prayer*. "The practice of the Jesus Prayer incorporates some ancient awareness of the body's role in prayer, a premodern understanding that can help us with re-integration [of the body and the mind]."

She describes how reintegration happens to her when she begins praying the Jesus Prayer:

> In the usual course of things, going through the day, my awareness is usually buzzing at the top of my head—even above my head, it feels like, if I'm particularly stressed. . . . Even now I begin to see that if I stop the pointless buzzing and turn to Christ, I can feel my mind coming in for a landing.[99]

That "landing" leads away from an outward-facing orientation to a turning inward, toward a prayer generated down in the heart. This turning inward is particularly important during a time when the competition for our attention is fierce, and we face a strong daily, hourly, or even minute-by-minute temptation to scatter our attention outwardly rather than concentrate it inwardly in prayer.

Albert Rossi, a professor to seminarians and future pastors in pastoral counseling, offers a surprising first step toward becoming a healing presence in his book by that title. The first step in his view is cultivating inner silence and stillness through the use of the Jesus Prayer. By using arrow prayers, we can cultivate a heart that allows God to work through us and be a healing presence to others. "We can have joy come from within us," he writes. "We can be suffused with joy by God's grace. To *suffuse* means to spread over or through something, to fill, to saturate, to permeate, to imbue. We saturate the space we occupy through the light of joy."[100] Repeating arrow prayers allows joy to spread through us and offer light to others. Thus, arrow prayers can turn us outward as well as inward.

On the advice of her father of confession, my friend Nardeen prays short Jesus Prayers for "all those around me during my commute, at work, for each customer or patient I deal with, while walking in the hallways of my workplace, to keep Christ constantly before my eyes and have him bless everyone I meet and everywhere I go." Arrow prayers serve to both turn us inward to God, but also outward to those who need our prayers and for whom we intercede.

These friends learned about arrow prayers from their spiritual fathers, as I have. For Nardeen and I, our fathers of confession also serve as spiritual fathers, giving guidance and advice as well as taking our confessions. Some Christians have a confessor as well as a spiritual father, the latter serving as a mentor and offering advice but not hearing confessions. The arrow prayer practice is often "handed down" by a confessor, a spiritual father, or another elder or mentor. Sometimes it is also modeled by saintly people in our lives, such as our parents and grandparents.

My friend Peter shared with me how he picked up the practice of paraphrasing Psalm 121:8, changing it to the first person and present tense, whenever leaving or returning home: "The Lord watches over my coming out and my going in both now and forevermore." His maternal grandmother, who was a constant presence in his life since she emigrated to the US from Egypt, prayed this and other arrow prayers often. According to Peter, "Her relationship with God and the saints was personal, in that she would be speaking to them constantly as if conversing with a person next to her." Many Christians build personal relationships with the saints, acknowledging that the saints are part of the "church victorious," those who have already finished the race (see Hebrews 12:1), but who are still among us in spirit if not in the flesh, praying for us and hearing our requests for their prayers. Despite many tragedies in his grandmother's life, including the early death of her oldest son just as he was finishing pharmacy school, Peter notes that "she never fell into despair or lost the faith, but just relied wholly on God. That was her joy." Arrow prayers remind us of how much we rely on God, and that reliance, that ongoing connection, that encounter, brings joy.

Mary, a fellow member of an online mother's group, shared a unique verse she used as an arrow prayer during a particularly difficult time in her life when she was going through a divorce: "This is the day the LORD has made; We will rejoice and be glad in it" (Psalm 118:24). She explained that she prays this verse "when I have an inclination to feel indignant or disappointed with the circumstances, when I am in a season of despondency." She looked to God for joy during one of the most difficult times in her life, and he met her there.

If hospitality helps us heal from the loneliness of our earthly sojourn, arrow prayers fuel us along the way. Metropolitan Anthony Bloom likens these prayers as "a background, a walking-stick, throughout the day and throughout life."[101] Arrow prayers remind us that even when we are alone, we are really never alone. We are surrounded by a team, an ethereal community, a great cloud of witnesses (see Hebrews 12:1). We can reach the Creator of the universe with one sentence prayed from our anxious, weary, aching hearts, shooting up like an arrow to his own heart. He sends us back "stabs of joy," in the words of C. S. Lewis. He sends his angels, as well as the saints in heaven and on earth who regularly intercede for us with prayers and tears. God is with us; we are never alone. All we need to do is call upon him. In his presence "*is* fullness of joy" (Psalm 16:11).

Arrow prayers and praying the Hours are intimately connected. Praying the Hours regularly allows us to engrave the Psalms in our hearts and gives us an arsenal of arrow prayers in times of need. The Twelfth Hour prayer, for example, includes these verses from the Psalms, all of which I have used as arrow prayers at different times:

Out of the depths I have cried to You, O Lord;
Lord, hear my voice!

Let Your ears be attentive To the voice of my supplications.
(Psalm 130:1–2)

Though I walk in the midst of trouble, You will revive me.
(Psalm 138:7)

Lord, I cry out to You; Make haste to me!
Give ear to my voice when I cry out to You.
(Psalm 141:1)

When these verses are repeated daily, they build a reserve to draw upon for their spontaneous use. Spontaneity is not a reliable way to develop an arrow prayer habit, however. Most people, when they are guided to use arrow prayers, are also guided to the times to use them, such as Nardeen's praying for her patients in the hospital halls during the night shift, or my prayers to calm anxious thoughts before bed. Some spiritual fathers advise praying a certain number of arrow prayers (usually the Jesus Prayer) per day, designating a time and using a prayer rope, prayer beads, or a rosary to help count them. This deliberate practice allows them to arise more naturally as we go through our days and find ourselves in times of need.

I find arrow prayers especially helpful when I am angry. Anxiety and fear often go hand and hand with anger, and anger can rise up in ways that are not conducive to relationships, especially to raising children. Anger and fear are passions and most certainly joy thieves. In the heat of the moment, I can certainly count backward from ten to keep my voice down, but I can also ask God for his mercy (I usually do both). I have found that those instances of wanting to yell in anger are fewer and farther between when I am intentional about daily praying arrow prayers. Praying this way has also given me a tool for helping my children manage their own strong emotions. When my children were younger, unable to control their tempers or in the middle of a meltdown, I would hold them tightly in my arms and tell them, "Take a deep breath and say the Jesus Prayer with me." Now that they are older, I might ask them to sit quietly somewhere and pray some arrow prayers. (They'll still get a hug.)

I've also read my children two books from a series called *The Silent Way* by Jeanette Aydlette and Marilyn Rouvelas.[102] *Peter Clashes with Anger* and *Eleni Looks at Jealousy* each tackle a joy thief (a "passion"), and each child goes through a conversation with his or her grandfather about how to overcome that passion, namely through practicing stillness. Hand in hand with the practice of stillness are arrow prayers, and the grandpa advises each grandchild to find a place to sit quietly and pray, "Lord have mercy."

When I drafted this chapter, it was snowing outside, and my children were playing with blocks in the living room. I took that moment, observing them, to pause and pray a few arrow prayers: "My Lord Jesus Christ, thank you for these children." I thought about my husband still at church. "My Lord Jesus Christ, bring my husband home safely in this snow." My toddler hit his older brother with a toy. Before intervening, I prayed, "My Lord Jesus Christ, Son of the Living God, have mercy on me, a sinner."

Near bedtime we pray a shortened Twelfth Hour prayer from the *Agpeya* as a family. The absolution prayer of that Hour requests, "For the sake of your Holy Name, Lord, and for Your goodness and Your love to mankind, forgive us those sins we have committed this day, whether they are by action, by word, by thought or any of our senses. *Grant us a peaceful night free of all anxiety*" (emphasis mine).

Arrow prayers have always been my companion before bed, helping me remove anxious thoughts from my mind. My father of confession gave me that advice many years ago when I complained of struggles to fall asleep because of all the thoughts running through my head. Now, as my oldest child asks me how to fall asleep more easily, I give him the same advice—pray an arrow prayer. Some nights, I pray aloud a few repetitions of the Jesus Prayer with him, and then fall silent. Eventually he falls asleep, but I sometimes stay there, still praying.

PUT JOY INTO PRACTICE

I've shared a number of arrow prayers above that have been used by believers for centuries. I invite you to choose one or more of these and to begin to use them, or perhaps add another one to your existing prayers. To make it easier, I'll list them here:

Lord have mercy

My Lord Jesus Christ, Son of God,
have mercy on me, a sinner.

My Lord Jesus Christ, Son of the Living God,
have mercy on me, a sinner.

Save me, O God!
For the waters have come up to *my* neck.
(PSALM 69:1)

Lord, teach me to do Thy will.

Lord, as you will, and as you know, have mercy.

Lord, help!

Be willing to help me, O Lord, because I am weak and cannot keep up this battle.

Lord Jesus, protect me against my tongue.

Make haste, O God, to deliver me! Make haste to help me, O Lord! (Psalm 70:1)

This *is* the day the Lord has made; we will rejoice and be glad in it. (Psalm 118:24)

My Lord, Jesus Christ, son of the Living God, give me patience.

Let all adverse powers be banished beneath the sign of the image of the cross.

The Lord watches over my coming out and my going in both now and forevermore.
(*see* Psalm 121:8)

Out of the depths I have cried to You, O Lord; Lord, hear my voice! Let Your ears be attentive *to* the voice of my supplications. (Psalm 130:1–2)

Though I walk in the midst of trouble, You will revive me. (Psalm 138:7)

Lord, I cry out to You; Make haste to me! Give ear to my voice when I cry out to You.
(Psalm 141:1)

Many people use prayer ropes or beads in conjunction with arrow prayers to keep track of the number they've repeated. The tactile sense of the knot between one's fingers helps reduce distractions and focus the mind on the words of the prayer. A spiritual father or mentor might advise a certain number of arrow prayers to be prayed in a day intentionally. Prayer ropes can contain anywhere from thirty-three knots to five hundred, with most having one hundred knots. Sometimes, if I don't have a prayer rope or prayer beads on hand, I simply touch my thumb to each segment of my other four fingers, which adds up to twelve repetitions.

I invite you to pray twelve repetitions of the most often used arrow prayer together now. While most other forms of prayer usually imply standing, kneeling, or bowing, arrow prayers can be prayed in any position. With your eyes closed and your thumb keeping track of each repetition, pray:

My Lord Jesus Christ, Son of the Living God,
have mercy on me, a sinner.

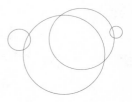

PRACTICE *Seven*

Singing Praise to God

Oh, God, to know you is life.

To serve You is freedom.

To praise you is the soul's joy and delight. . . .

When large numbers of people share

their joy in common, the happiness of each is greater

because each adds fuel to the other's flame.

    —St. Augustine of Hippo[103]

Joy delights in joy.

    —Shakespeare, Sonnet VIII

David Kipping, assistant professor of astronomy at Columbia University, studies universes hundreds of light-years away from the earth. At his Cool Worlds lab, he and other researchers discovered Kepler-167e, a planet outside our own solar system, about the size of Jupiter, and a thousand light-years away. "The exhilaration you feel from an act of discovery is joyous," he says. "Whether it's some little thing nobody else knew or an entirely new planetary system, you want to go out in the world and tell everyone. It's like being in love."[104] I cannot imagine the joy Kipping and his fellow scientists must feel at seeing these planets for the first time, but I do have a sense of wonder about the universe—a sense of awe at how deep and wide it is, and how little we know about it, despite how much we have discovered.

I think back to people living in ancient times and consider how they viewed the skies. Many years ago, on a trip to Kenya, I remember lying on my back in a field that was part of an orphanage in Maseno, a village outside the city of Kisumu. There, near the equator and away from the big city lights, I gazed in awe at the Milky Way above me. All I could think of was how God created this, and the words of the ancient psalmist came to mind: "When I consider Your heavens, the work of Your fingers, The moon and the stars, which You have ordained, What is man that You are mindful of him, And the son of man that You visit him?" (Psalm 8:3–4). Judging from all the mythology surrounding the stars and the number of psalms glorifying God for his wonders, the ancients must often have looked to the skies in awe.

In *The Jesus Prayer*, Frederica Mathewes-Green writes of us needing "a course in remedial awe." Comedian Jill Shargaa gave a humorous TED Talk in 2014 about our misuse of the word *awesome*. "There's no dynamic, there [are] no highs and lows, if everything is awesome," she says.[105] In an age of hyperbole, when a sandwich is awesome and a Tweet an outrage, many of us have lost the ability and the joy of recognizing the truly awesome.

But it might only take a few minutes of looking up toward the sky. Our daily concerns, worries, and fears keep us looking down, drawn away from what is praiseworthy all around us and above us.

While our technologies may be helpful, the online competition for our attention often draws our gaze from what truly deserves our attention. Photographing a brilliant night sky with a smart-phone just can't capture it. It can't capture the breathtaking sense of wonder and joy of the true experience. And it won't capture the sense of awe at the Creator of all this grandeur.

With a few exceptions, almost everyone who has observed the heavens in all their splendor cannot help feeling the presence of God. On the Apollo 8 mission in 1968, astronaut Frank Borman read the first ten verses of Genesis as he watched the earth rise from the moon's orbit. Buzz Aldrin brought bread and wine with him so that he could partake of the Eucharist as he and Neil Armstrong became the first men to walk on the moon. Astronaut James Irwin, as he watched the earth become smaller and smaller, said, "Seeing this has to change a man, has to make a man appreciate the creation of God and the love of God."[106] Irwin's words are reflected in the Psalms, although the psalmist likely never observed the earth the way Irwin did. The Psalms take this wonder a step further. The wonders of creation do not just inspire us to praise God; nature itself praises God.

"The heavens declare the glory of God; and the firmament shows His handiwork," Psalm 19 begins. "The seas have lifted up their voice," proclaims Psalm 93:3 (NIV). Sometimes the psalmist exhorts creation to praise its Creator: "Let the heavens rejoice, and let the earth be glad; Let the sea roar, and all its fullness; Let the field be joyful, and all that *is* in it. Then all the trees of the woods will rejoice before the LORD" (Psalm 96:11–13). "Let the rivers clap *their* hands; let the hills be joyful together before the LORD" (Psalm 98:8–9).

While we have talked about praying the Psalms when pray-ing the Hours, and looking to the Psalms for inspiration when giving thanks to God, it's now also important to recognize that psalms are songs—they are meant to be sung, and sung together as a community in praise to God. Thomas Staubli writes in the article "Performing Psalms in Biblical Times" that we actually know little about the Psalms being used for personal devotion among the Israelites before Christ, but we do know that they were sung communally in festive processions.[107] Throughout the centuries, the Psalms have inspired church hymnology, and they continue to be used in songs of worship and praise in diverse traditions. The Psalms as song help us experience the joy that comes from the practice of singing praise to God, especially if we can practice it as a community.

This is one of my favorite hymns of praise, sung communally at church during weekly Midnight Praises (*Tasbeha*):

The heavens declare the glory, of God until this day,
O you angels whom He has made,
praise Him and exalt Him above all.

Now all you powers of the Lord, bless His honored name,
O sun and moon and all the stars,
praise Him and exalt Him above all.

And also you rain and dew, sing praises unto our Savior,
for He is the God of our fathers,
praise Him and exalt Him above all

Glorify the Lord O clouds and winds,
together with the souls and the spirits,
O you cold and fire and heat,
praise Him and exalt Him above all.[108]

You also nights and days, light and darkness and lightning,
glorify the Lover of Mankind,
praise Him and exalt Him above all.

You trees and all that springs on the earth,
and all that moves in the sea, mountains and the forests,
praise Him and exalt Him above all.

Praise without ceasing, the Lord the King of the kings,
O you rivers and seas,
praise Him and exalt Him above all.

The heavens, the angels, the sun, the moon, the stars, the rain
and dew, the clouds and winds, the souls and the spirits, cold, fire
heat, nights and days, light, darkness, and lightning, trees and all
plants, anything in the sea that moves, mountains, forests, rivers
and seas—all of these are called to praise God with us.

The practice of praising God takes us beyond the awe of his
creation to the joy of praising him who made and redeemed it.
"Proclaim with a voice of joy . . . praise Him and exalt Him above
all," the hymn continues. In raising our voices in praise together,
we trample on the enemy that tempts us to turn away from God.
When we focus on God and not ourselves, we are uplifted from the
worries and concerns of this world that draw us away from the joy
of the Resurrection. In the words of the Resurrection Psalmody:

In the eve of the Sabbath, the women could only weep
and cry and wail. Yet in the dawn of the Sabbath, the
weeping was postponed and the wailing has ceased. For
the great joy of the Resurrection of the Logos has nullified
all mourning.[109]

The exposition above, which is read during the Midnight Praises of the Holy Fifty Days[110] after the Resurrection, refers to the "eve of the Sabbath." Members of the Jewish community prepare for Sabbath with a flurry of work—preparation for a day of rest during which those tasks cannot be done. In her book *Mudhouse Sabbath* Lauren Winner quotes Nan Fink's description of Sabbath preparations:

> On Friday afternoon, at the very last minute, we'd rush home, stopping at the grocery to pick up supplies. Flying into the kitchen we'd cook ahead for the next twenty-four hours. Soup and salad, baked chicken, yams and applesauce for dinner, and vegetable cholent or lasagna for the next day's lunch.[111]

It seems like our modern lives are characterized by this rushing about, working, preparing—but without stopping to partake of a true day of rest the way the Sabbath is supposed to be kept. Winner explains what this rest looks like from the Jewish perspective: "You are commanded, principally, to be joyful and restful on Shabbat, to hold great feasts, sing happy hymns, dress in your finest."[112] When we succumb to the busyness of life—another joy stealer—it makes it even harder for us to experience the joy of the Resurrection.

The joy of the Resurrection does not merely give us rest from work. It takes us beyond this day of rest into a new day—the eighth day—when the cycle of life, work, rest, and finally death is broken by the power of the Resurrection. We look forward now not to eternal rest but to eternal *life*, a life in God's presence, where we cannot refrain from the praises overflowing from our lips in his presence and where there is fullness of joy.

What greater way to confess and acknowledge God's presence than a gathering of singing praise? The act of singing itself physiologically has been proven to lift our spirits by filling our lungs with oxygen—with life. Singing also releases endorphins and oxytocin, two hormones related to feelings of pleasure, trust, and bonding.[113] Singing in groups offers even more benefits. Research from the University of East Anglia has recently shown "a combination of singing and social engagement gave participants a feeling of belonging and well-being that often lasted a day or more, as well as improved social skills and confidence."[114] The popularity of Handel's *Messiah* sing-ins in Europe and the US during the Christmas season is a testament to the joy people feel when they gather together to sing familiar songs of praise. Gospel choirs sing songs of praise using much repetition so everyone participating can join in boisterous song. Long before the benefits of singing were scientifically proven, believers were gathering together to lift up their voices in hymns and songs of praise.

Songs of praise focus on God and his greatness, with very little in the way of litany or supplication. Communal singing of praise is an opportunity to set aside our worries and concerns and focus instead on the greatness of God—in whose shadow those worries and concerns shrink. In my church, the congregation gathers for the purpose of praising God in a weekly service called *Tasbeha*, the Midnight Praises. In other churches this is also called Vigil. While this praise service can be done daily (as it is in the monasteries), it is most often practiced in church congregations on Saturdays, right after Vespers and before the celebration of the Divine Liturgy the next day.[115] Like the Hours, it requires no clergy, and draws from the Psalms and other Scripture as the people gather together to sing praises to the Lord of Hosts in preparation for his presence at the Eucharist a few hours later. In the words of Fr. Tadros Malaty, "Praise prepares us for enjoyment of the Eucharist, and the Eucharist propels us towards unceasing daily praise."[116]

I cannot imagine any situation more worrisome (and terrifying!) than being thrown into the fiery furnace the way the three saintly youth were because of their refusal to worship anyone or anything except the Living God. Yet as they are about to be thrown into the fire as per the Babylonian king's orders, they declare that their God will save them—and even if he does not, they will never bow down to the idols (see Daniel 3:17–18). When they are thrown into the fire, they are seen with a fourth person walking among them, unbound, who "is like the Son of God" (Daniel 3:25). This person is no longer visible when Shadrach, Meshach, and Abednego emerge from the furnace untouched.

The joy of the Lord's presence starts *in* that fiery furnace, not outside it. As Bishop Metthaous writes, "There is no resurrection without the cross, no victory without a battle."[117] Thus the "Hymn of the Three Saintly Youth" during *Tasbeha* begins: "O sing unto Him who was crucified, buried and resurrected, who trampled and abolished death, praise Him and exalt Him above all." We begin the hymn with an exhortation to the youth in the fire to sing to the Son of God who is there with them in their suffering—and therefore also in their joy. This exhortation applies to us as well. We don't wait to praise God until after we are saved from the furnace, when our prayers are answered the way we hope they will be. We praise him even in our troubles, acknowledging and confessing that he is there with us in those troubles. When we can wipe away from our eyes the smoke of our problems and praise him, we see him in his glory there—and this is powerful. This is joy.

Before the Midnight Praises begin, we start by praying the Midnight Hour. The Gospel of the First Watch is the Parable of the Ten Virgins. As the parable goes, all ten virgins were waiting with the lamps to receive the bridegroom when he arrived. The five wise virgins had enough oil in their lamps to see him, but the foolish ones did not. So the foolish ones asked the wise ones to give them some of their oil. The wise ones could not (see Matthew 25:1–13). I remember Madeleine L'Engle exclaiming in a creative writing class I took with her, "Why couldn't they just give them some oil!" For the longest time I asked myself the same question, notwithstanding the fact that this was a parable rather than a historical event.

I found my answer in the words of St. Seraphim of Sarov. The oil was the Holy Spirit, and the wise virgins had "acquired the Spirit." The Holy Spirit is everywhere and fills all, but only those who have acquired it can let their lamps shine brightly to receive the bridegroom. When we ask the Holy Spirit to dwell within us, it is God's gift to give, not ours. In the words of St. Augustine, "See, I have oil. But did I create the oil? It is a gift of God." Thus the five wise virgins could not share their oil, and the foolish ones needed only to accept the gift of God to keep their lamps burning. St. Seraphim points out that both the wise and foolish virgins had done good deeds, but:

> [T]he oil is not the good deeds, but the grace of the All-Holy Spirit of God which is obtained through good deeds and which changes souls from one state to another—such as, from a corruptible state to incorruptible state, from spiritual death to spiritual life, from darkness to light, from the stable of our being (where the passions are tied up like dumb animals and wild beasts) into a temple of the Divinity, the shining bridal chamber of eternal joy in Christ Jesus our Lord, the Creator, Redeemer and eternal Bridegroom of our souls.[118]

This parable opens the Midnight Watch to lead us into a few more hours of praise that almost seems excessive, luxurious. We could, after all, be outside doing, working, producing, serving, giving to the poor, feeding the hungry, visiting the sick. Why spend so many hours on a Saturday night just praising God, only to come back again on Sunday morning? The Gospel reading of the Second Watch gives us our answer:

> And behold, a woman in the city who was a sinner, when she knew that Jesus sat at the table in the Pharisee's house, brought an alabaster flask of fragrant oil, and . . . she kissed His feet and anointed *them* with the fragrant oil. (Luke 7:37–38)

Simon, Christ's host, protests that this woman touching him is a sinner, and Christ explains to him that the one who has been forgiven less loves less, but the one who has been forgiven more loves more. In Mark 14, we read of a similar anointing in the home of another host named Simon, perhaps the same one:

> As He sat at the table, a woman came having an alabaster flask of very costly oil of spikenard. Then she broke the flask and poured *it* on His head. But there were some who were indignant among themselves, and said, "Why was this fragrant oil wasted? For it might have been sold for more than three hundred denarii and given to the poor." And they criticized her sharply. (Mark 14:3–5)

Our praise to God is like this flask of fragrant oil, worth perhaps a lifetime of wealth, poured out excessively and recklessly on the feet of the Savior. Time is life, our portion regardless of our financial circumstances. An hour is an hour whether you are rich or poor, and an hour that is spent praising God is a gift, a sacrifice to offer to the one who has forgiven us much, enabling us to love much. It is, in Christ Jesus's eyes, "a beautiful thing" (Mark 14:6, NIV).

After the Midnight Watch, the hour of expectation, is prayed, the Midnight Praises begin with this hymn: "Arise, O Children of the Light." We, by keeping watch, enter into the joy of the bridegroom and the wedding feast, where, in God's presence, we magnify and exalt him. The link between Vespers, Praises, and the Eucharist services here becomes clear. In Vespers we pray litanies, in the Praises we praise God with a joyful psalm, and in the Liturgy, we partake of the wedding feast.

On that long-ago visit to Kenya, I also remember going to Nairobi and visiting Africa's largest slum, Kibera. I remember holding the hands of some young children as we skipped across little creeks of open sewage. Along with some local deacons, I visited the homes of sick people, of families who had not been to church in some time, of neighbors who invited us to visit their tin-roof homes while we were there. After we visited with people, we would invite them to join us for a meeting in a building within the slum. There, we all gathered and shared some Bible readings and meditations. At the closing prayer, the Kenyans began to sing a simple song in Swahili: *Hakuna Mungo kama Wewe, hakuna Mungo kama Wewe, hakuna Mungo kama Wewe, Ewe Mungo Wongu. Nasema asante, nasema asante, nasema asante, Ewe Mungo Wangu.* "There is no other God like you, there is no other God like you, there is no other God like you, you are my God, my God. So we say thank you, Lord, so we say thank you, Lord, so we say thank you, Lord, you are my God, my God."

Their harmonic voices singing this simple song of praise transformed the bare walls of that shantytown building into a heavenly place. And there, in that setting with few material possessions, much sickness, much hunger, and much pain, the people gathered together in praise and thanked God for being God. In the bright city lights of bustling Nairobi, it was much harder to see the Milky Way—but in that darkness they didn't need to see the stars. They saw God himself.

My mind is still on those five foolish virgins, but there is hope for them too. For the Parable of the Ten Virgins is a parable of the kingdom, and the Liturgy is the kingdom of heaven on earth. And so, as long as there is today, we still have time to acquire the Spirit, light the darkness, and arise to praise the Lord again, rejoicing together with our lips, putting joy into practice.

PUT JOY INTO PRACTICE

While we can always sing praises to God during our personal prayers and devotions, the full joy of praising God is found in gathering together and singing as a community. Almost every religious tradition has some form of this gathering, whether it is the dedicated vigil of Midnight Praises or a part of Sunday morning worship.

But songs of praise can be sung anywhere, at any time, and it is not hard for two or three to gather to do so. I invite you to take advantage of some other opportunities to sing songs of praise to God together:

- As a family, choose a favorite hymn of praise and sing it together during prayer.

- While visiting a sick person, bring the lyrics of a song of praise with you, perhaps one familiar to the person you are visiting, and sing it together if you can.

🔖 When inviting others into your home in hospitality, share a song of praise together, and add the joy of praising God to the joy of receiving him into your home.

🔖 If your tradition has a dedicated service of praise, like Vigil or Midnight Praises, participate in the service when it is held. Revive it if it is not being held.

I invite you to sing this praise to God:

Let us give thanks
Unto Christ our God
With David the Prophet
And the Psalmist.

For he has made the heavens
And all its hosts
And established the earth
On the waters.

These two great stars
The sun and the moon
He has made to enlighten
The firmament.

He brought forth the winds
Out of His treasure box
He breathed unto the trees
And they blossomed.

He caused the rain to fall
Upon the face of the earth
And it sprouted
And gave its fruit.

He brought forth water
Out of a rock
And gave it to His people
In the wilderness.

He made man
In His image
And His likeness
That he may praise Him.

Let us praise Him
And exalt His name
And give thanks to Him:
His mercy endures forever.

—PSALI ADAM for the Second Canticle, Midnight Praises

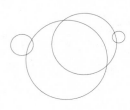

xios! Axios! Axios! Worthy! Worthy! Worthy!" they sang joyously as the plane landed at Cairo International Airport on May 14, 2018. Bishops, deacons, laypeople, and airline employees all standing on the tarmac, cymbals clanging. When the Axios hymn was done, they continued with the Resurrection hymn *Christos Anesti* ("Christ is risen from the dead, trampling death by death, and granting life to those who are in the tombs"), and then another Resurrection hymn, *Nikhoros Tirou,* sung in Arabic ("All you heavenly orders, sing to our God with the melody of praise, rejoice with us today with gladness, in the Resurrection of the Lord Christ. . . . He has granted us the everlasting joy, and freed us from bitter bondage). The doors of the plane opened, and hymns continued, louder now. One by one, twenty wooden coffins were rolled out. The Coptic Orthodox Church was welcoming the return of the Coptic martyrs of Libya.[119]

The hymns continued as the coffins were organized in rows of seven on the airport tarmac. One bishop was given a microphone to speak, and he spoke of joy. He spoke of the strength of faith each of these young men bore when they were kidnapped, facing certain death at the hands of ISIS because of their Christian faith. Their execution was broadly televised in February 2015. He spoke of how they stood strong, even as they saw their brothers in Christ, one after the other, mercilessly beheaded. Another bishop spoke, sharing how proud these martyrs made the Coptic Orthodox Church. "They have raised our heads," he said, using an Arabic phrase that translates as "they did us proud," "and now we can walk with our heads held high." A third bishop likened the joyful arrival of their bodies to the celebration of the return of the relics of St. Mark the Evangelist to Egypt in 1969. A fourth pointed out how these young men's relics returned to Egypt not only during the Holy Fifty Days of the Resurrection Feast, but also on the eve of the commemoration of another famous Egyptian saint who defended the faith against the heretics: St. Athanasius of Alexandria.

It had taken over three years for their bodies to be repatriated to Egypt from Libya. Those three years involved rigorous negotiations between governments and intelligence services. It involved transporting the bodies to Italy, where DNA testing confirmed their identities for their families. Finally the bodies arrived in Egypt, where they would be taken to their resting place in the village of al-Our, Minya, Egypt, where their families could visit them and pilgrims could request their prayers.

His Holiness Pope Tawadros II, the 118th successor of St. Mark the Apostle and St. Athanasius the Apostolic, arrived at the airport. When he reached the coffins lined up on the tarmac, he stood for a moment, taking in the sight. I wondered what his thoughts were at that moment. He then walked forward and went to each coffin, lifting the flowers to read the name. He put his hand, which was holding a cross, on the coffin after he read the name and said some words. I imagine he said each name, perhaps also asking each martyr to pray for him. Finally he reached the rest of the bishops, and after the Lord's Prayer, he began praying the Thanksgiving Prayer. He then continued by praying the Litany of the Departed:

> Graciously, O Lord, repose all their souls in the bosom of our holy fathers Abraham, Isaac and Jacob. Sustain them in a green pasture, by the water of rest in the Paradise of joy, the place out of which grief, sorrow and groaning have fled away in the light of Your saints. . . . As for those, O Lord, whose souls You have taken, repose them, and may they be worthy of the kingdom of

the heavens. As for us all, grant us our Christian perfection that would be pleasing to You, and give them and us a share and an inheritance with all Your saints.

Finally, the *Axios* hymns began again as the coffins were transported to the cars that would take the martyrs' bodies to their hometown. In what might be the longest funeral procession in history, the twenty coffins were driven about five hours from Cairo to Minya, where their families and their village waited to greet them with the same joyful hymns that were sung at the airport. This reception was even more festive, as an *Axios* was sung for each martyr by name, the women ululated, the drivers honked their horns to the tune of a wedding procession, and the people fought to touch each coffin and get a blessing from each martyr. Their bodies were laid to rest in a newly built church dedicated to their memory.

"Why are they happy?" my daughter asked. "Don't they have moms and families who are sad that they died?"

"They are happy," I explained, "because this isn't the end. Do you hear what they are singing?"

"*Christos Anesti?*"

"*Christos Anesti*. Christ is risen. Death is not the end anymore. And these men, specifically, died as witnesses for Christ. They did for him what he did for us. He died for us; they died for him. So they get a special crown in heaven, and white robes."

"So there's nothing in those coffins?"

"Their bodies are in those coffins, but their souls are with God. And they will be united again at the resurrection of the dead, when Jesus comes again."

"So they are all squishy in heaven right now?"

"Well, that part I don't know."

There is a lot we don't know. But what we do know is that an airplane landing with twenty coffins would never be met with such a joyous celebration if we did not believe in the resurrection of the dead.

> If in this life only we have hope in Christ, we are of all men the most pitiable. But now Christ is risen from the dead, *and* has become the first fruits of those who have fallen asleep. For since by man *came* death, by Man also *came* the resurrection of the dead. For as in Adam all die, even so in Christ all will be made alive. But each in his own order: Christ the firstfruits, afterward those *who are* Christ's at His coming. (1 Corinthians 15:19–23)

The joy of the Resurrection is for those who belong to Christ, for the twenty-one martyrs of Libya, and for all who live every day, not in death but in life, not in fear but in courage, not in shame but in victory.

Our family live-streamed the events in Egypt on our computers in the USA, far from the daily possibility of dying for our faith but still faced with the daily decision of putting our joy into practice. Fr. Alexander Schmemann defines a Christian as "the one who, wherever he looks, finds Christ and rejoices in Him. And this joy transforms all his human plans and programs, decisions and actions, making all his mission the sacrament of the world's return to Him who is the life of the world."[120]

The practices we've discussed in this book all center around finding Christ through personal and communal spiritual practices. While visiting the sick and offering hospitality are most obviously communal practices, praying the Hours, arrow prayers, repentance, thanksgiving, and singing praise should all be practiced interpersonally and in community even as they are practiced individually. These are not the only ways to put joy into practice, but they are certainly a start that can lead to discovering other ways to joy.

There are six Sundays during the Holy Fifty Days of the Resurrection, and those Sunday Gospel readings give us the chance to get to know our Savior again as the resurrected Lord. Passages that were read before the Feast of the Resurrection take on a new light when read during the Holy Fifty Days, the church still adorned in white and the hymns still sung joyously. Each reading reacquaints us with Christ.

We begin with Thomas Sunday, reading from John:19–31, when Christ appears to Thomas and allows him to touch his hands and his side, confirming that the one who was crucified is indeed risen and sparking his joyous profession of faith, "My Lord and My God!" The reading concludes with, "These are written that you may believe that Jesus is the Christ, the Son of God, and that believing you may have life in His name" (John 20:31). What is this life in his name? The next four readings explain.

On the second Sunday, the reading from John 6:35–45 reminds us that Jesus is the Bread of Life. "He who comes to Me shall never hunger, and he who believes in Me shall never thirst." We receive the bread of life at the Eucharist in thanksgiving, and we also receive it after the liturgy, when we, being filled with him, open our doors in hospitality so that others might also be filled. On the third Sunday, the reading from John 4:1–42 brings us back to the woman at the well, reminding us that Jesus is the Living Water. It reminds us also of the joy of repentance, casting off our old waterpots so we can receive the water that he gives, the "fountain of water springing up into everlasting life" (John 4:14) we can share with others so they also have life in his name.

On the fourth Sunday, Christ reminds us that because he is "the light of the world" (John 8:12), those who believe in him will not live in darkness. Not only that, but he tells us, "You are the light of the world," and says, "Let your light so shine before men, that they may see your good works and glorify your Father in heaven" (Matthew 5:14, 16). These good works are the sweet fruit of the Holy Spirit, the joy we offer to the world as Christians when we pour ourselves out in service to others.

Mother Erene of Blessed Memory once shared this story about a monk known as "the one with a needle and thread":

> Whenever this monk saw one of his brothers [the other monks] with torn clothes, he would sew them. This was his main occupation. When he grew older, having struggled and about to depart the world, he told them, "I want the key to the door of Paradise." The monks brought him the icon of our Lord Jesus Christ. He was happy to see it and embraced it.
>
> But he said again, "I want the key to the door of Paradise." So they brought him the icon of the Virgin, the Mother of God. He was happy to see and embraced it.
>
> But once more, he said, "I want the key to the door of Paradise." One of the monks said, "Bring him a needle and thread." They did. So, he was very happy and told them, "These are the keys to the door of Paradise."[121]

I imagine that this monk, while sewing for his brothers, prayed arrow prayers for them, serving them with prayers and with his hands. It is a story reminiscent of Abba Macarius's grapes. When, during the fifth Sunday, Jesus tells us, "I am the way, the truth, and the life" (John 14:6), it is his way of self-emptying and self-sacrifice that we are called to follow, as this monk did; it is Christ's truth—Christ's person, not some philosophical ideal, as this monk imitated—and his life, the everlasting life we have because of his cross and resurrection, the life this monk knew he would inherit with his needle and thread. In the words of the Coptic hymn for the Feast of the Cross, "Through His cross/and His holy resurrection/He returned man once more/to the Paradise." We enter Paradise not just by looking at Christ's image in an icon, but by being icons of Christ himself.

Finally, the sixth Sunday of the Holy Fifty Days falls four days after the Feast of the Ascension. If we have imagined ourselves with all the believers who saw him face-to-face after his resurrection, being reminded that he is the bread of life, the water of life, the light of the world, the way, the truth, and the life, now we imagine ourselves looking up to him as he ascends to his Father after promising his Holy Spirit, but not before he exhorts us with these words: "In the world you will have tribulation; but be of good cheer, I have overcome the world" (John 16:33). Other translations say "take heart" or "take courage." Christ has conquered the world, and he is willing to give us all we need to conquer it with him. In fact, all we must do is ask: "Ask, and you will receive, that your joy may be full" (16:24).

Our joy will be complete when we ask from him all we need to live the joy of the Resurrection. There is no promise of an easy life; practicing the joy of the Resurrection in this life will lead to struggles, tribulation, persecution, and even death, the way it did for the twenty-one martyrs of Libya, all who have come before them, and all who will come after them.

For those of us not facing certain death, we face tribulation of a different kind—trying to practice true joy in a world that tempts us with shiny imitations. The world offers us connection, but only the superficial kind when we surround ourselves with those who make us comfortable rather than reaching out to do what is uncomfortable. It offers us longer life in the form of new medications, fad diets, and fitness clubs, but none of those can offer us eternal life. It offers us new cars, new gadgets, more possessions, more to consume when we tire of what we have already consumed—possessions we cannot take with us to eternity that weigh us down here on earth. It feeds our passions, our "joy thieves," rather than helping us master them. It offers us "inner peace" through spiritual practices divorced from the Spirit, but it doesn't give us true peace. We will face tribulation when we fight off these imitations, when we refuse to succumb and instead, with Christ, we overcome.

Perhaps most of us have succumbed to these temptations at one point or another, believing these joy imitators to be the "fullness of joy" that God's presence promises us. We then find ourselves spent, exhausted, and joyless, making the world around us wonder how different these Christians are from everyone else.

It is my hope that in our continual practice of joy, we can become "credible witnesses" again. Movies and documentaries continue to be produced, trying to find the "historical" Jesus, combing early texts and new archeological findings to understand him and figure out how Christianity possibly could have spread so widely. While they devote lots of energy to scholarly, historical, and academic pursuits, they skirt around the elephant in the room: the Resurrection. Perhaps they do so because they do not see Christians living the joy of the Resurrection, so they seek to find some other reason Christianity spread so fast, how a lowly carpenter is believed by millions to be the King of kings—some other reason besides the most obvious: that he rose from the dead.

The producers of these documentaries skirt around the Resurrection because they can't find any "empirical evidence" of it. And they won't find any, because they are looking in all the wrong places, trying to find evidence in scrolls found in the depths of the desert, in tombs, in the accounts of people who actually are dead, in ruins. No living person will be found by seeking "the living among the dead" (Luke 24:5). If they want to find out if Jesus is alive, they will have to go where he is—with the people who believe in him and see him everywhere.

Those who want to find Jesus will find him in the desert, for sure, but not in desert scrolls. He'll be found in the arid, unlivable Egyptian desert where thousands of Christian monastics have built their homes and communities around him. Jesus will be found in the tombs, for sure, but not in the empty tomb where he was buried. Instead he will be found in the places believers frequent to remember that their dead loved ones will rise again as he has risen—such as the church in al-Our, Minya. He will be found not just in the accounts of dead historians like Josephus, but in the accounts of living Christians who strive to live with him despite all the obstacles, despite the ease of life they would have if they didn't follow him, and even despite the real possibility of dying for him. In the words of C. S. Lewis, "If Christianity was something we were making up, of course we could make it easier."[122] Jesus will be found in the ruins, but not the ruins of archeological digs. He'll be found in the ruins of people's lives as he helps rebuild them. I hope that those looking for Jesus Christ will find him in the community of believers and in the behavior of those Christians.

I'm blessed to look around at my church congregation and see Christ there. It has been five years since that Resurrection night I wrote of in the introduction to this book. Andrew is still singing hymns, still giving bear hugs, and still inspiring all of us with his joy. Michelle's family started a foundation in her honor to carry on her legacy by supporting youth like her. The woman with three children is still bringing her mother to church when she can, and she still photographs her when she takes Communion.

It has taken me about five years to write this book, not just because of the research I had to do or because I had to write it in the margins of motherhood, work, and service. It also took time because I had to live it myself. I believe that Jesus is risen, but I sometimes don't behave that way. There were periods when I stopped writing, not for lack of time, but because I was not being at all joyful. I was succumbing to the imitation joy offered by the world. I was allowing the passions, the joy thieves, to steal my joy. How could I write a book about putting joy into practice when I was not practicing it myself? I remember the comment by our priest in the invitation: having joy is not easy.

What brought me back to writing, of course, was the reminder to take my own advice. Some arrow prayers often opened the way, a whispered psalm, a visitor to share a meal with, a prayer of repentance for a cold heart, an evening of prayer, a phone call to a friend who had a loved one in the hospital . . . any one of those led to another, until I was tasting again of the fruit of the Spirit.

These practices are not meant to burden you with more activities to add to an already full plate, but they do require time. However, making time for such things has been shown to increase the available time we have for the things we want to do, not just the things we have to do. Time management experts point to this reality all the time. Once we recognize that we have more time, we start to see the space open up before us to engage in the other practices that help us experience joy—opening our doors to others in hospitality, visiting the sick, and gathering with the believers to sing praise to God. I cannot see any wiser investment of time than in investing it in those practices that help us give and receive sacrificial love—to help us live in joy.

My hope is that, by drawing from examples of how my church helps us live in the joy of the Resurrection, this book might open your eyes to the ways your tradition helps you practice joy. Once you begin to see it, whether you are in a happy situation or in great pain, it is all joy.

. . . [Jesus Christ], whom having not seen you love. Though now you do not see *Him*, yet believing, you rejoice with joy inexpressible and full of glory, receiving the end of your faith—the salvation of *your* souls."

(1 Peter 1:8–9)

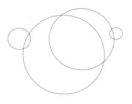

GIVING THANKS, PART II

This book would not be possible without the blessing of being part of the congregation of St. Antonious & St. Mina Coptic Orthodox Church in East Rutherford, New Jersey, especially those members who have allowed me to share their stories. I am inspired by your struggles and your joy in the Resurrection. Thank you.

For my friends on and off social media, who also generously shared their stories about practicing joy, especially those who shared their experiences with arrow prayers, hospitality, and praises, thank you.

For Fr. Athanasius Farag, who is my father and my teacher in more ways that I can count, and for my mother, Soher Farag, who modeled joy for me, thank you.

For Fr. Antonious Makaryus, Fr. Tadros Malaty, Fr. Youhanna Abadeer, and Fr. Bishoy Andrawes, my fathers of confession at different times of my life and my spiritual fathers all the time, thank you.

For my husband, Fr. Bishoy Mikhail, who shared stories, resources, and ideas, who encouraged me and supported me, and who carried our household as I finished drafts of this book, despite his own overwhelming responsibilities as a priest, thank you.

To Allison Backous Troy, Mariam El-Shamaa, Maria Andrawis, Traci Rhoades, His Grace Bishop Suriel, Fr. Anthony Messeh, Fr. Michael Sorial, Fr. Peter Farrington, Laura Michael, Mireille Mishriky, Donna Alamanian Risk Asdourian, and Martha Farag—thank you for reading all or part of this manuscript, for your early endorsements, and most of all for your feedback. Thank you for making this book immensely better than what it was before your input.

For my friends and family who offered support, encouragement, and resources, helping carry my load (whether they knew it or not), Mary Farag and Fr. Joseph Gall, Merrell Sami, Jessica Ryder-Khalil, Joseph and Nelly Mata, Bassem Narouz, Martha Farag, Ramya El-Salah, Mary Ibrahim, Janine El-Gamal, Marianne and Antony Farag, thank you.

For Jon Sweeney, who pushed me to make this book more accessible and immeasurably better than it was when he read it first, thank you.

For the entire team at Paraclete Press and their efforts in publishing and marketing this book, thank you.

For the creators of *PBS Kids, Horrid Henry, Dino Dan and Dino Dana, Fireman Sam, Thomas the Tank Engine, Paw Patrol, the Swiss Family Robinson,* and all the cartoons and movies that occupied my children so I could complete this manuscript without too much guilt about the extra screen time, thank you.

For Bishop Thomas, who knew I would be a writer, thank you.

No endeavor is ever carried out alone, and I ask forgiveness of anyone whose name I have overlooked. You made this book possible—I cannot thank you enough.

1 In the Coptic Orthodox Church of Alexandria, we refer to Holy Week as Pascha Week.

2 Kim Parker and Eileen Patten, "The Sandwich Generation: Rising Financial Burdens for Middle-Aged Americans," January 30, 2013, *Pew Research Center*; http://www.pewsocialtrends.org/2013/01/30/the-sandwich-generation/

3 Fr. Tadros Yacoub Malaty, *Introduction to the Coptic Orthodox Church* (St. George's Coptic Orthodox Church, Alexandria, Egypt, 1993), 247.

4 The liturgical calendar of the Coptic Orthodox Church of Alexandria begins with the month of Tute, which falls on September 11 or 12 on the Gregorian calendar. For more information about the Coptic Calendar, see Wassef, Cérès Wissa, "Calendar, Months of Coptic," *Claremont Coptic Encyclopedia*; http://ccdl.libraries.claremont.edu/cdm/ref/collection/cce/id/407.

5 Dennis Okholm, *Dangerous Passions, Deadly Sins: Learning from the Psychology of Ancient Monks* (Grand Rapids, MI: Brazos, 2014), 5.

6 Quoted by Everett Ferguson in *Inheriting Wisdom: Readings for Today from Ancient Christian Writers* (Peabody, MA: Hendrickson Publishers, 2004), 61.

7 Samuel, Bishop, *The Road to Happiness*, sermons translated and published by St. Mark's Coptic Orthodox Church, Chicago, IL, 2001, on the 25th anniversary of his departure on October 6, 1981, when he was killed during the assassination of Egyptian President Anwar El-Sadat.

8 C. S. Lewis. *Surprised by Joy: The Shape of My Early Life*, (New York: HarperCollins, 2010), Kindle Edition, 125–126.

9 Quoted by the Dalai Lama and Desmond Tutu in *The Book of Joy: Lasting Happiness in a Changing World* (New York: Penguin Publishing Group, 2016), 245.

10 Lois Farag, *Balance of the Heart: Desert Spirituality for Twenty-First Century Christians* (Eugene, OR: Cascade Books, 2012), 118.

11 Okholm, *Dangerous Passions, Deadly Sins*, 15.

12 Lindsay Holmes, "People Who Swear May Be Happier, Healthier and More Honest," *Huffington Post* (February 2018); https://www.huffingtonpost.com/entry/health-benefits-of-swearing_us_5a5e44a8e4b0106b7f65b3a6.

13   C. S. Lewis, *Surprised by Joy: The Shape of My Early Life* (New York: HarperOne, 2017), 265.

14   Cal Newport, *So Good They Can't Ignore You: Why Skills Trump Passion in the Quest for Work You Love* (New York: Grand Central Publishing, 2012).

15   Elizabeth Gilbert, "Choosing Curiosity Over Fear," *On Being with Krista Tippett* (July 2016); https://onbeing.org/programs/elizabeth -gilbert-choosing-curiosity-over-fear/.

16   Farag, *Balance of the Heart,* 78.

17   Dalai Lama and Desmond Tutu, *The Book of Joy: Lasting Happiness in a Changing World* (New York: Penguin Publishing Group, 2016), 12.

18   Antoine de Saint-Exupéry, *The Little Prince.* Richard Howard, trans. (New York: Houghton Mifflin Harcourt, 2000), 61

19   Traditionally, Christians face the East when praying because, in the words of St. John of Damascus, "Since, therefore, God is spiritual light, and Christ is called in the Scriptures Sun of Righteousness and Dayspring, the East is the direction that must be assigned to His worship. For everything good must be assigned to Him from Whom every good thing arises." "Concerning Worship Towards the East"; http://www.ccel.org/ccel/schaff/npnf209.iii.iv.iv.xii.html.

20   Fr. Antonious Makaryus is the beloved and longtime parish priest of St. Mary and St. Antonious Coptic Orthodox Church in Queens, New York, where I spent part of my childhood.

21   Archbishop Basilios, "The Canonical Book of Hours," *Claremont Coptic Encyclopedia,* Aziz Atiya, ed.; http://ccdl.libraries.claremont.edu/cdm/ singleitem/collection/cce/id/413/rec/1

22   Mike Aquilina and Christopher Bailey, *Praying the Psalms with the Early Christians: Ancient Songs for Modern Hearts.* (Frederick, MD: Word Among Us Press, 2009), 9.

23   See "Field Notes on Praying the Hours," February 2018, (http:// www.tracesoffaith.com/blog/2018/02/field-notes-on-praying-the -hours.html), and "Praying the Hours (What is that?)" March 2018 (http://www.tracesoffaith.com/blog/2018/03/praying-the-hours -what-is-that.html).

24   His Holiness Pope Shenouda III of Blessed Memory (3 August 1923–17 March 2012) was the 117th Pope of Alexandria and the See of St. Mark from 1971 to his departure in 2012. His forty years as pope saw the rapid expansion of the Coptic diaspora. He was a

gifted speaker and a prolific writer. More information about him can be found at http://www.copticchurch.net/topics/pope/.

25 "A Lesson in Prayer," June 2009, http://jenniferfulwiler.com/2009/06/a-lesson-in-prayer/.

26 paragraph 14, http://www.athanasius.com/psalms/aletterm.htm

27 *Make the Words Your Own: An Early Christian Guide to the Psalms* (Brewster, MA: Paraclete Press, 2014), xxii.

28 Sophfronia Scott and Tain Gregory, *This Child of Faith: Raising a Spiritual Child in a Secular World* (Brewster, MA: Paraclete Press, 2018), 95.

29 *This Child of Faith*, 96.

30 "Transforming Habits of Spiritual People, Part 1 of 3," January 24, 2018; http://www.stgeorgeministry.com/transforming-habits-spiritual-people-pt-1-3/.

31 Isaac (Bishop of Ninevah), *The Ascetical Homilies of St. Isaac the Syrian* (Brookline, MA: Holy Transfiguration Monastery. 2011) ,151.

32 Dietrich Bonhoeffer, *Psalms: The Prayer Book of the Bible* (Minneapolis: Augsburg Fortress, 1970), 64–65.

33 Quoted in Fr. Tadros Malaty, *Let's Enjoy the Gift of Joy and Avoid the Trap of Lethal Sorrow*, Berta Youssef, Salwa Wahba, Keren Fonseco, trans. (South Brunswick, NJ: Queen Mary & Prince Tadros Coptic Orthodox Church, 2014), 4.

34 Rich Cohen, "Sugar Love: A not so sweet story," *National Geographic Magazine* (August 2013); http://ngm.nationalgeographic.com/2013/08/sugar/cohen-text.

35 Bishop Metthaous, *The Spirituality of the Praise According to the Rite of the Coptic Orthodox Church* (Sydney, Australia: Coptic Orthodox Diocese of Sydney, 1980).

36 Fr. Tadros Y. Malaty and Bishoy Boshra Fayez, *An Invitation to the Happy Life* (South Brunswick, NJ: The Queen St. Mary and Prince Tadros Coptic Orthodox Church), 13–14.

37 Fuligni Telzer, et al, "Neural Sensitivity to Eudaimonic and Hedonic Rewards Differentially Predict Adolescent Depressive Symptoms over Time," *Proceedings of the National Academy of Sciences of the United States of America*, 2014 May 6; 111(18): 6600–6605; https://www.ncbi.nlm.nih.gov/pmc/articles/PMC4020059/.

38 Bishoy Abba, *The Coptic Synexarion*; http://www.copticchurch.net/topics/synexarion/bishoy.html.

39 Quoted in Malaty, *Let's Enjoy the Gift of Joy and Avoid the Trap of Lethal Sorrow,* 4.

40 Martha Farag, "Reflections on Being a Woman of Steel," *Stupidity and Humility,* Monday, April 14, 2014, http://stupidityandhumility .blogspot.com/2014_04_01_archive.html.

41 Albert Rossi, "Welcome to Our First Episode," *Becoming a Healing Presence,* September 1, 2011; http://www.ancientfaith.com/podcasts/ healingpresence/welcome_to_our_first_episode

42 Patti Neighmond, "To Ease Pain, Reach for Your Playlist," *National Public Radio;* https://www.npr.org/sections/health- shots/2015/06/22/415048075/to-ease-pain-reach-for-your-playlist -instead-of-popping-a-pill.

43 Tim Vivian, ed., *Becoming Fire: Through the Year with the Desert Fathers and Mothers* (Collegeville, MN.: Liturgical Press, 2008), 163.

44 St. Athanasius, *Festal Letter 7,* NPNF, s. 2, v. 4, 1256, quoted in *The Great Lent: Patristic Meditations on the Sunday Gospels, Treasures of the Fathers of the Church, Volume II* (Diamond Bar, CA.: St. Paul Brotherhood Press, 2010), 122.

45 Fr. Tadros Malaty, *Patristic Commentary on the Gospel of John,* 300, 301, quoted in *The Great Lent: Patristic Meditations on the Sunday Gospels. Treasures of the Fathers of the Church, Volume II,* 175.

46 St. Augustine, *Tracate on John,* Tracate 15, NPNF, s. 1, v. 7. Quoted in *The Great Lent: Patristic Meditations on the Sunday Gospels. Treasures of the Fathers of the Church, Volume II,* 166.

47 Origen, *Commentary on John,* bk. 13:43–51, 181, 201–217. Quoted in *The Great Lent: Patristic Meditations on the Sunday Gospels. Treasures of the Fathers of the Church, Volume II.* (Diamond Bar, Calif.: St. Paul Brotherhood Press, 2010), 171.

48 Origen, *The Great Lent,* 172.

49 Gus George Christo, translator, *The Fathers of the Church Patristic Series* (Washington, DC: Catholic University of America Press, 2005) Volume 96, Homily 8, 115.

50 Pope Shenouda, *The Life of Repentance and Purity* (Crestwood, NY: St. Vladimir's Seminary Press, 2013), 22.

51 "Synaxarion of St. Photini and Those Martyred with Her," 26 February 2016; https://www.johnsanidopoulos.com/2016/02/ synaxarion-of-saint-photini-samaritan.html

52 Fr. Tadros Malaty, *How to Stay Repentant?,* Dr. Samir Migally, ed. (South Brunswick, NJ: Queen Mary & Prince Tadros Coptic Orthodox Church, 2014), 1.

53 Malaty, *How to Stay Repentant?* 2.

54 Bishop Kallistos Ware, *The Orthodox Way.* (Crestwood, NY: St. Vladimir's Seminary Press, 1995). 44.

55 His Holiness Pope Tawadros II is the 118th Pope and Patriarch of Alexandria and the See of St. Mark. In 2013 by election, he succeeded His Holiness Pope Shenouda III, the 117th Pope, who departed in 2012.

56 Justin Martyr, *First Apology;* https://www.ccel.org/ccel/schaff/anf01 .viii.ii.ii.html.

57 Fr. Boules George, "A Message to Those Who Kill Us," Laura Michael of Coptic Dad & Mom, trans., http://www .copticdadandmom.com/fr-boules-george/.

58 A version of this section of Practice Four was originally published as "Suffering Is Part of the Calling" on my blog, *Being in Community,* in May 2017 at http://beingincommunity.com/suffering-is-a-part-of-the-calling/.

59 "Gratitude Is Good Medicine," UC Davis Health, 25 November 2015; http://www.ucdmc.ucdavis.edu/welcome/ features/2015-2016/11/20151125_gratitude.html.

60 Colby Itkowitz, "The Science Behind Why You Shouldn't Stop Giving Thanks after Thanksgiving," *Washington Post,* 22 November 2017; https://www.washingtonpost.com/news/inspired-life/ wp/2016/11/24/the-science-behind-why-you-shouldnt-stop-giving -thanks-after-thanksgiving/.

61 Michael Hyatt, *Your Best Year Ever: A Five Step Plan for Reaching Your Most Important Goals* 2018. Ada, MI: Baker Books, 2018), 92.

62 Liz Becker, "Why Mothers Need to Stop Calling Themselves #Blessed," April 26, 2018; https://motherwellmag.com/2018/04/26/ perspective-why-mothers-need-to-stop-calling-themselves-blessed/.

63 Jana Riess, *Flunking Sainthood: A Year of Breaking the Sabbath, Forgetting to Pray, and Still Loving My Neighbor* (Brewster, MA: Paraclete Press, 2011), 108.

64 *Flunking Sainthood,* 110.

65 Fr. Beniameen Morgan, *The Eucharist: A Journey of Repentance. A Revised and Expanded Edition* (Giza, Egypt: St. Mark the Apostle's Books, 2010), 79.

66 Dr. Angela Gorrell, associate research scholar at the Yale Center for Faith & Culture, addresses the pastoral use of social media in more depth in "Rejoicing and Mourning Online," *Faith and Leadership,* April 2018; https:// www.faithandleadership.com/angela-gorrell-rejoicing-and-mourning-online.

67 Archbishop Basilios, "Offertory." *The Claremont Coptic Encyclopedia.* Aziz Atiya, ed., Vol. 6. http://ccdl.libraries.claremont.edu/cdm/ singleitem/collection/cce/id/1479/rec/3.

68   Fr. Athanasius Iskander, *Understanding the Liturgy: A series of articles published by Father Athanasius Iskander in Parousia, September 1993 – March 1997* (Kitchener, Ontario: St. Mary Coptic Orthodox Church, 2001).

69   Paulo Freire, *Pedagogy of the Oppressed* (New York: Continuum, 2000), 45.

70   Pope Shenouda III, *Contemplations on the Prayer of Thanksgiving and Psalm 51(50)* (Sydney, Australia: Coptic Orthodox Publication and Translation, 1998), 16.

71   Richard Louv, *Last Child in the Woods: Saving Our Children from Nature-Deficit Disorder* (Chapel Hill, NC: Algonquin Books, 2005).

72   Rowan Williams, *Being Christian: Baptism, Bible, Eucharist, Prayer* (Grand Rapids, MI: Eerdmans, 2014), 48.

73   *The Divine Liturgy of the Armenian Church*, http://www.armenianchurchlibrary.com/files/The_Divine_Liturgy-English.pdf.

74   Farag, *Balance of the Heart*, 102.

75   *On the Incarnation of the Word*, 2.8.

76   *On the Incarnation of the Word*, 2.9.

77   Benedicta Ward, SLG, translator, *The Sayings of the Desert Fathers: The Alphabet Collection* (Collegeville, MN: Liturgical Press, 1984), 17–18, 128.

78   Amy G. Oden, *And You Welcomed Me: A Sourcebook on Hospitality in Early Christianity* (Nashville: Abingdon Press, 2001), 76.

79   Ward, *The Sayings of the Desert Fathers*, xxiv.

80   More extensive information on St. Pachomius and his *koinonia* can be found at Armand Veilleux, "Pachomius, Saint," *The Claremont Coptic Encyclopedia*, Ateya Aziz, ed., 1991, http://ccdl.libraries.claremont.edu/cdm/ref/collection/cce/id/1497

81   Farag, *Balance of the Heart*, 244.

82   Oden, *And You Welcomed Me*, 64.

83   Oden, *And You Welcomed Me*, 62.

84   St. Cyril of Alexandria, *Commentary on the Gospel of St. Luke* (Long Island, NY: Studion Publishers, 1983), 292.

85   *The Paraclete Book of Hospitality* (Brewster, MA: Paraclete Press, 2012), 77.

86   APA Staff, "Loneliness: A Growing Health Concern." *American Psychiatry Association*, January 5, 2017; https://www.psychiatry.org/news-room/apa-blogs/apa-blog/2017/01/loneliness-a-growing-health-concern.

87   George Monbiot, "The town that's found a potent cure for illness—community." *The Guardian*. 21 Feb 2018, https://www.theguardian.com/commentisfree/2018/feb/21/town-cure-illness-community-frome-somerset-isolation.

88 Juliana Schmemann, *The Joy to Serve* (Montreal, Québec: Alexander Press, 2009), 54.

89 Amy G. Oden, *God's Welcome: Hospitality for a Gospel-Hungry World* (Cleveland, OH: The Pilgrim Press, 2008), 24.

90 Also known as St. Menas; more information can be read about him here: http://www.learn.columbia.edu/treasuresofheaven/saints/Menas.php.

91 Fr. Marcus Bishay, *The Life of Prayer According to the Coptic Orthodox Church* (Burr Ridge, IL: St. Mark Coptic Orthodox Church, 2001).

92 Lois Farag, *Balance of the Heart: Desert Spirituality for Twenty-First Century Christians*, 140.

93 Irénée Hausherr, *The Name of Jesus: The Names of Jesus Used by Early Christians, The Development of the "Jesus Prayer."* (Kalamazoo, MI: Cistercian Publications, 1978), 211.

94 *Conferences*, 10.10.5.

95 Hausherr, *The Name of Jesus*, 206.

96 Quoted in Hausherr, *The Name of Jesus*, 130.

97 Farag, *Balance of the Heart*, 144–145.

98 Fr. Matta Al-Maskeen. *Guidelines to Prayer* (Scetis, Egypt: The Monastery of St. Macarius the Great), 15.

99 Frederica Mathewes-Green, *The Jesus Prayer: The Ancient Desert Prayer That Tunes the Heart to God* (Brewster, MA: Paraclete Press, 2009), 101–102.

100 Albert S. Rossi, PhD, *Becoming a Healing Presence* (Chesterton, IN: Ancient Faith Publishing, 2014), 79.

101 Anthony Bloom, *Beginning to Pray.* (Mahwah, NJ: Paulist Press, 1970), 60.

102 Published by Holy Cross Orthodox Press, 2012; available on Amazon through third-party sellers only or through the publisher's website, holycrossbookstore.com.

103 St. Augustine quotes, https://staugny.org/quotes.

104 Bill Retherford, "Brave New Worlds," *Columbia Magazine*, Winter 2017; http://magazine.columbia.edu/features/winter-2017/brave-new-worlds.

105 Jill Shargaa, "Please, Please People, Let's Put the Awe Back in Awesome," July 2014; https://www.ted.com/talks/jill_shargaa_please_please_people_let_s_put_the_awe_back_in_awesome.

106 Rebecca Rosen, "Communion on the Moon: Religious Experience in Space," *The Atlantic*, July 16, 2012; https://www.theatlantic.com/technology/archive/2012/07/communion-on-the-moon-the-religious-experience-in-space/259826/.

107 Thomas Staubli, "Performing Psalms in Biblical Times," *Biblical Archaeology Review*, Washington, Vol. 44, Iss. 1, (Jan/Feb 2018): 62.

108 Psali Watos for the Three Saintly Youth (Greek). https://tasbeha .org/hymn_library/view/109; many of the lyrics are based on Daniel 3:51–80 as found in the Septuagint.

109 Exposition of the Resurrection Evening – Batos Exposition.

110 Special hymns are added to the Midnight Praises according to the liturgical season.

111 Lauren F. Winner, *Mudhouse Sabbath: An Invitation to a Life of Spiritual Discipline—Study Edition* (Brewster, MA: Paraclete Press, 2009), Kindle edition.

112 Winner, *Mudhouse Sabbath.*

113 Sarah Horn, "Singing Changes Your Brain," *Time*, August 16, 2013; http://ideas.time.com/2013/08/16/singing-changes-your-brain/.

114 University of East Anglia, "How Singing Your Heart Out Can Make You Happier," *Science Daily*, December 21, 2017; https://www .sciencedaily.com/releases/2017/12/171221101402.htm.

115 For a complete description of the rite of Midnight Praises in the Coptic Orthodox Church, see the "Service of the Psalmodia" section in Roberston, Muftah, et al, "Music, Coptic." *The Claremont Coptic Encyclopedia.* Aziz Suriel Atiya, ed. 1991. http://ccdl.libraries .claremont.edu/cdm/ref/collection/cce/id/1446.

116 Fr. Tadros Malaty, *Praise (Tasbeha), the Vespers, and the Matins: Sharing in Angelic Worship.* Dr. Maged S. F. Mikhail, Trans., (Jersey City, NJ, St. Mark's Coptic Orthodox Church,1995).

117 Bishop Metthaous, *The Spirituality of the Praise: According to the Rite of the Coptic Orthodox Church.* Coptic Orthodox Diocese of Sydney, Australia.

118 St. Seraphim of Sarov, On the Acquisition of the Holy Spirit, https://www.fatheralexander.org/booklets/english/sermon_st_ seraphim.htm

119 The twenty-first martyr was from Ghana, and it is presumed that his body was also returned to his country.

120 Alexander Schmemann, *For the Life of the World: Sacraments and Orthodoxy* (Crestwood, NY: St. Vladimir's Seminary Press, 1963), 112.

121 From *Tamav Erene, Leader and Mother in the Monastic Pastures*, published by the Monastery of St. Mercurius in Old Cairo, Egypt, 2011.

122 C. S. Lewis, *Mere Christianity* (New York: HarperOne, 2003), 158.

ABOUT PARACLETE PRESS

WHO WE ARE

As the publishing arm of the Community of Jesus, Paraclete Press presents a full expression of Christian belief and practice—from Catholic to Evangelical, from Protestant to Orthodox, reflecting the ecumenical charism of the Community and its dedication to sacred music, the fine arts, and the written word. We publish books, recordings, sheet music, and video/DVDs that nourish the vibrant life of the church and its people.

WHAT WE ARE DOING

BOOKS | PARACLETE PRESS BOOKS show the richness and depth of what it means to be Christian. While Benedictine spirituality is at the heart of who we are and all that we do, our books reflect the Christian experience across many cultures, time periods, and houses of worship.

We have many series, including *Paraclete Essentials; Paraclete Fiction; Paraclete Poetry; Paraclete Giants;* and for children and adults, *All God's Creatures,* books about animals and faith; and *San Damiano Books,* focusing on Franciscan spirituality. Others include *Voices from the Monastery* (men and women monastics writing about living a spiritual life today), *Active Prayer,* and new for young readers: *The Pope's Cat.* We also specialize in gift books for children on the occasions of Baptism and First Communion, as well as other important times in a child's life, and books that bring creativity and liveliness to any adult spiritual life.

The Mount Tabor Books series focuses on the arts and literature as well as liturgical worship and spirituality; it was created in conjunction with the Mount Tabor Ecumenical Centre for Art and Spirituality in Barga, Italy.

MUSIC | THE PARACLETE RECORDINGS label represents the internationally acclaimed choir *Gloriæ Dei Cantores,* the *Gloriæ Dei Cantores Schola,* and the other instrumental artists of the *Arts Empowering Life Foundation.*

Paraclete Press is the exclusive North American distributor for the Gregorian chant recordings from St. Peter's Abbey in Solesmes, France. Paraclete also carries all of the Solesmes chant publications for Mass and the Divine Office, as well as their academic research publications.

In addition, PARACLETE PRESS SHEET MUSIC publishes the work of today's finest composers of sacred choral music, annually reviewing over 1,000 works and releasing between 40 and 60 works for both choir and organ.

VIDEO | Our video/DVDs offer spiritual help, healing, and biblical guidance for a broad range of life issues including grief and loss, marriage, forgiveness, facing death, understanding suicide, bullying, addictions, Alzheimer's, and Christian formation.

Learn more about us at our website:
www.paracletepress.com
or call us toll-free at 1-800-451-5006.

SCAN
TO
READ
MORE

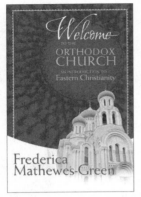
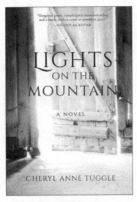
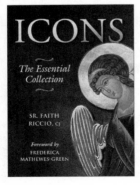